HOW TO
MAKE A
GEORGIA WILL

Fourth Edition

——

Edward P. Moses
Mark Warda
Attorneys at Law

SPHINX® PUBLISHING
AN IMPRINT OF SOURCEBOOKS, INC.®
NAPERVILLE, ILLINOIS

Fourth Edition, 2002

Published by: **Sphinx® Publishing, An Imprint of Sourcebooks, Inc.®**

<u>Naperville Office</u>
P.O. Box 4410
Naperville, Illinois 60567-4410
630-961-3900
Fax: 630-961-2168
http://www.sourcebooks.com
http://www.sphinxlegal.com

This publication is designed to provide accurate and authoritative information in regard to the subject matter covered. It is sold with the understanding that the publisher is not engaged in rendering legal, accounting, or other professional service. If legal advice or other expert assistance is required, the services of a competent professional person should be sought.
From a Declaration of Principles Jointly Adopted by a Committee of the
American Bar Association and a Committee of Publishers and Associations

This product is not a substitute for legal advice.
Disclaimer required by Texas statutes.

Library of Congress Cataloging-in-Publication Data
Moses, Edward P.
    How to make a Georgia Will / Edward P. Moses, Mark Warda.-- 4th ed.
        p. cm. -- (Legal survival guides)
    Includes index.
    ISBN 1-57248-180-3
    1. Wills--Georgia--Popular works. I. Warda, Mark. II. Title. III. Series.

KFG144.Z9 M67 2002
346.75805'4--dc21
                                                                    2001055007

Printed and bound in the United States of America.

VHG Paperback — 10 9 8 7 6 5 4 3 2 1

CONTENTS

HOW TO MAKE
A GEORGIA WILL

USING SELF-HELP
LAW BOOKS

Before using a self-help law book, you should realize the advantages and disadvantages of doing your own legal work and understand the challenges and diligence that this requires.

THE GROWING TREND

Rest assured that you won't be the first or only person handling your own legal matter. For example, in some states, more than seventy-five percent of divorces and other cases have at least one party representing him or herself. Because of the high cost of legal services, this is a major trend and many courts are struggling to make it easier for people to represent themselves. However, some courts are not happy with people who do not use attorneys and refuse to help them in any way. For some, the attitude is, "Go to the law library and figure it out for yourself."

We at Sphinx write and publish self-help law books to give people an alternative to the often complicated and confusing legal books found in most law libraries. We have made the explanations of the law as simple and easy to understand as possible. Of course, unlike an attorney advising an individual client, we cannot cover every conceivable possibility.

COST/VALUE ANALYSIS

Whenever you shop for a product or service, you are faced with various levels of quality and price. In deciding what product or service to buy, you make a cost/value analysis on the basis of your willingness to pay and the quality you desire.

When buying a car, you decide whether you want transportation, comfort, status, or sex appeal. Accordingly, you decide among such choices as a Neon, a Lincoln, a Rolls Royce, or a Porsche. Before making a decision, you usually weigh the merits of each option against the cost.

When you get a headache, you can take a pain reliever (such as aspirin) or visit a medical specialist for a neurological examination. Given this choice, most people, of course, take a pain reliever, since it costs only pennies; whereas a medical examination costs hundreds of dollars and takes a lot of time. This is usually a logical choice because it is rare to need anything more than a pain reliever for a headache. But in some cases, a headache may indicate a brain tumor and failing to see a specialist right away can result in complications. Should everyone with a headache go to a specialist? Of course not, but people treating their own illnesses must realize that they are betting on the basis of their cost/value analysis of the situation. They are taking the most logical option.

The same cost/value analysis must be made when deciding to do one's own legal work. Many legal situations are very straight forward, requiring a simple form and no complicated analysis. Anyone with a little intelligence and a book of instructions can handle the matter without outside help.

But there is always the chance that complications are involved that only an attorney would notice. To simplify the law into a book like this, several legal cases often must be condensed into a single sentence or paragraph. Otherwise, the book would be several hundred pages long and too complicated for most people. However, this simplification necessarily leaves out many details and nuances that would apply to special or unusual situations. Also, there are many ways to interpret most legal questions. Your case may come before a judge who disagrees with the analysis of our authors.

Therefore, in deciding to use a self-help law book and to do your own legal work, you must realize that you are making a cost/value analysis. You have decided that the money you will save in doing it yourself outweighs the chance that your case will not turn out to your satisfaction. Most people handling their own simple legal matters never have a problem, but occasionally people find that it ended up costing them more to have an attorney straighten out the situation than it would have if they had hired an attorney in the beginning. Keep this in mind if you decide to handle your own case, and be sure to consult an attorney if you feel you might need further guidance.

LOCAL RULES   The next thing to remember is that a book which covers the law for the entire nation, or even for an entire state, cannot possibly include every procedural difference of every county court. Whenever possible, we provide the exact form needed; however, in some areas, each county, or even each judge, may require unique forms and procedures. In our *state* books, our forms usually cover the majority of counties in the state, or provide examples of the type of form that will be required. In our *national* books, our forms are sometimes even more general in nature but are designed to give a good idea of the type of form that will be needed in most locations. Nonetheless, keep in mind that your *state*, county, or judge may have a requirement, or use a form, that is not included in this book.

You should not necessarily expect to be able to get all of the information and resources you need solely from within the pages of this book. This book will serve as your guide, giving you specific information whenever possible and helping you to find out what else you will need to know. This is just like if you decided to build your own backyard deck. You might purchase a book on how to build decks. However, such a book would not include the building codes and permit requirements of every city, town, county, and township in the nation; nor would it include the lumber, nails, saws, hammers, and other materials and tools you would need to actually build the deck. You would use the book as your guide, and then do some work and research involving such matters as whether you need a permit of some kind, what type and grade of wood are available in your area, whether to use hand tools or power tools, and how to use those tools.

Before using the forms in a book like this, you should check with your court clerk to see if there are any local rules of which you should be aware, or local forms you will need to use. Often, such forms will require the same information as the forms in the book but are merely laid out differently, use slightly different language, or use different color paper so the clerks can easily find them. They will sometimes require additional information.

CHANGES IN THE LAW
Besides being subject to state and local rules and practices, the law is subject to change at any time. The courts and the legislatures of all fifty states are constantly revising the laws. It is possible that while you are reading this book, some aspect of the law is being changed or that a court is interpreting a law in a different way. You should always check the most recent statutes, rules and regulations to see what, if any changes have been made.

In most cases, the change will be of minimal significance. A form will be redesigned, additional information will be required, or a waiting period will be extended. As a result, you might need to revise a form, file an extra form, or wait out a longer time period; these types of changes will not usually affect the outcome of your case. On the other hand, sometimes a major part of the law is changed, the entire law in a particular area is rewritten, or a case that was the basis of a central legal point is overruled. In such instances, your entire ability to pursue your case may be impaired.

Again, you should weigh the value of your case against the cost of an attorney and make a decision as to what you believe is in your best interest.

INTRODUCTION

This book was written to help Georgia residents quickly and easily make their own wills without the expense or delay of hiring a lawyer. It begins with a short explanation of how a will works and what a will can and cannot do. It is designed to allow those with simple estates to quickly and inexpensively set up their affairs to distribute their property according to their wishes. It includes an explanation of how such things as *joint property* and *pay on death* accounts will affect your planning.

It also includes information on appointing a guardian for any minor children you may have. This can be useful in avoiding bad feelings between relatives and in protecting the children from being raised by someone you would object to.

Chapters 1 through 7 explain the laws that affect the making of a will. The glossary will help you understand the legal forms used in this book. Appendix A contains sample filled-in will forms to show you how it is done. Appendix B contains blank will forms you can use. A flow chart in Appendix B will help you choose the right will form based upon your circumstances and desires.

You can prepare your own will quickly and easily by using the forms out of the book, by photocopying them, or retyping the material on sheets of paper. The small amount of time it takes to do this can give you and your loved ones the peace of mind of knowing that your estate will be distributed according to your wishes.

A surprising number of people have had their estates pass to the wrong parties because of a simple lack of knowledge of how the laws work. Before using any of the forms in Appendix B, you should read and understand all of the chapters of this book.

In each example given in the text you might ask, "What if the spouse died first?" or "What if the children are grown up?" and then the answer might be different. If your situation is at all complicated, you are advised to seek the advice of an attorney. In many communities, wills are available for very reasonable prices. No book of this type can cover every difference in every case, but a knowledge of the basics will help you to make the right decisions regarding your property.

The forms in this book are for simple wills to leave property to your family, or if you have no family, to friends or charities. As explained in Chapter 2, if you wish to disinherit your family and leave your property to others, you should consult with an attorney who can be sure that your will cannot be successfully *challenged*, or disputed, in court.

BASICS OF GEORGIA WILLS

1

Before making your will, you should understand how a will works and what it can and cannot do. Otherwise, your plans may not be carried out and the wrong people may end up with your property.

WILL DEFINED

A *will* is a document you can use to control who gets your property, who will be guardian of your children and their property, and who will manage your estate upon your death.

HOW A WILL IS USED

Some people think a will avoids *probate*, which is the court procedure for dispensing someone's property after death. It does not. A will is the document used in probate to determine who receives the property, and who is appointed *guardian* of your children and *executor* or *personal representative* of your estate.

AVOIDING
PROBATE

If you wish to avoid probate you need to use methods other than a will, such as joint ownership, pay-on-death accounts, or living trusts. The first two of these are discussed later in this chapter. For information on living trusts you should refer to a book that focuses on trusts as used for estate planning.

If a person successfully avoids probate with all of his or her property, then he or she may not need a will. In most cases, when a husband or wife dies no will or probate is necessary because everything is owned jointly. However, everyone should have a will in case he or she forgot to put some property into joint ownership. Or, some property that was received just prior to death, may not avoid probate for some reason. Both husband and wife may even die in the same accident.

JOINT TENANCY AND PROBATE

Property that is owned in *joint tenancy with right of survivorship* does not pass under a will. If a will gives property to one person but it is already in a joint account with another person, the will is usually ignored and the joint owner of the account gets the property. This is because the property in the account avoids probate and passes directly to the joint owner. A will only controls property that goes through probate. There are exceptions to this rule. If money is put into a joint account only for convenience, it might pass under the will. However, if the joint owner does not give it up, it could take an expensive court battle to get it back.

Putting property into joint tenancy does not give absolute rights to it. If the estate owes estate taxes, the recipient of joint tenancy property may have to contribute to the tax payment. Also, some states give spouses a right to property that is in joint accounts with other people. This is explained later in this chapter.

Example 1: Ted and his wife want all of their property to go to the survivor of them. They put their house, cars, bank accounts, and brokerage accounts in joint ownership. When Ted dies his wife only has to show his death certificate to get all the property transferred to her name. No probate or will is necessary.

Example 2: After Ted's death, his wife, Michelle puts all of the property and accounts into joint ownership with her son, Mark. Upon Michelle's death, Mark needs only to present her death certificate to have everything transferred into his name. No probate or will is necessary.

JOINT TENANCY AND YOUR WILL

If all property is in joint ownership or if all property is distributed through a will, things are simple. But when some property passes by each method, a person's plans may not be fulfilled.

Example 1: Bill's will leaves all his property to his sister, Mary. Bill dies owning a house jointly with his wife, Joan, and a bank account jointly with his son, Don. Upon Bill's death Joan gets the house, Don gets the bank account and his sister, Mary, gets nothing.

Example 2: Betty's will leaves half her assets to Ann and half her assets to George. Betty dies owning $1,000,000 in stock jointly with George, and a car in her name alone. Ann gets only half the value of the car. George gets all the stock and the other half of the value of the car.

Example 3: John's will leaves all his property equally to his five children. Before going in the hospital he puts his oldest son, Harry, as a joint owner of his accounts. John dies and Harry gets all of his assets. The rest of the children get nothing.

In each of these cases the property went to a person it probably should not have because the *decedent* (the person who died) did not realize that joint ownership overruled his or her will. In some families this might not be a problem. Harry might divide the property equally (and possibly pay a gift tax). But in many cases Harry would just keep everything and the family would either never talk to him again, or would take him to court.

Joint Tenancy Risks

In many cases joint property can be an ideal way to own property and avoid probate. However it does have risks. If you put your real estate in joint ownership with someone, you cannot sell it or mortgage it without that person's signature. If you put your bank account in joint ownership with someone they can take out all of your money.

Example 1: Alice put her house in joint ownership with her son. She later married Ed and moved in with him. She wanted to sell her house and to invest the money for income. Her son refused to sign the deed because he wanted to keep the home in the family. She was in court for ten months getting her house back and the judge almost refused to do it.

Example 2: Alex put his bank accounts into joint ownership with his daughter Mary to avoid probate. Mary fell in love with Doug who was in trouble with the law. Doug talked Mary into "borrowing" $30,000 from the account for a "business deal" that went sour. Later she "borrowed" $25,000 more to pay Doug's bail bond. Alex did not find out until it was too late that his money was gone.

Tenancy in Common and Probate

In Georgia there are two basic ways to own property, joint tenancy with right of survivorship and tenancy in common. *Joint tenancy with right of survivorship* means that if one owner of the property dies, the survivor automatically gets the decedent's share. *Tenancy in common* means when one owner dies, that owner's share of the property goes to his or her heirs or beneficiaries under the will.

Example 1: Tom and Marcia bought a house together and lived together for twenty years but were never married. The deed did not specify joint tenancy. When Tom died, his brother inherited his half of the house and it had to be sold because Marcia could not afford to buy it from him.

Example 2: Lindsay and her husband Rocky bought a house. When Rocky suddenly died, Lindsay obtained full ownership of the house by filing a death certificate at the courthouse. That was because the deed to the house stated that they were husband and wife so ownership was presumed to be *tenancy by the entireties.*

A Spouse and Your Will

Unlike in some other states, under Georgia law a surviving spouse cannot overrule a will properly executed that is consistent with public policy. The person making the will can leave his or her real or personal property to strangers and exclude a spouse and children. However, the next section explains an exception.

Your Spouse, Your Minor Children, and Support

Under Georgia law, unlike some other states, you may exclude your spouse from your will. However, Georgia law does have provisions for spousal support and child support.

This is called *support for one year* and it requires timely application to the probate court. In some instances such support can be extended past one year but the whole concept of one year support poses legal questions that exceed the scope of this book and should be discussed with an attorney.

I/T/F Bank Accounts versus Joint Ownership

One way of keeping bank accounts out of your estate and still retain control over them is to title them *in trust for* or I/T/F with a named beneficiary. Some banks may use the letters POD for *pay on death* or TOD for *transfer on death*. Either way the result is the same. No one except you can get the money until your death, and on death it immediately goes directly to the person you name, without a will or probate proceeding. These are sometimes called *Totten Trusts* after the court case that declared them legal.

Example: Rich opened a bank account in the name of "Rich, I/T/F Mary." If Rich dies, the money automatically goes to Mary. Prior to his death Mary has no control over the account, does not even have to know about it, and Rich can take Mary's name off the account at any time.

Securities Registered as I/T/F

A new law has been passed in over half the states that allows people to register their *securities*, such as stocks, bonds, and mutual funds in the I/T/F form. This allows them to pass immediately upon death to the beneficiaries without the need for probate.

Unfortunately, Georgia has not yet passed this law, but you can still take advantage of it. If your mutual fund or brokerage account is with a company in one of the states that allows such registrations, you can set up an I/T/F account even though Georgia has not yet passed the law. Check with your broker or mutual fund. If they cannot offer you an I/T/F account, perhaps it would be worth changing to one who does to avoid probate.

MARRIAGE AND YOUR WILL

If you get married you should either make out a new will or sign a *codicil* after the wedding, which explains whether or not you plan to change the terms of the will. (A codicil is an attachment to a will that changes parts of the will. It must be executed in the same manner as a will.) Otherwise your will may be declared invalid.

Example: John made out his will leaving everything to his physically-challenged brother. When he married Joan, an heiress with plenty of money, he did not change his will because he still wanted his brother to get his estate. When he died, Joan received John's entire estate, and John's brother got nothing.

DIVORCE AND YOUR WILL

A judgment of divorce automatically *revokes* (makes invalid) your will unless it is clear in the will that the divorce was thought about when written. If your will did not contemplate divorce you should not rely on this automatic revocation to exclude your spouse. If you die with a will naming your ex-spouse, there may be a delay and legal fees if he or she tries to insist on a share of your estate.

CHILDREN AND YOUR WILL

If you have a child or adopt a child after making your will and do not rewrite it, your will can be revoked.

Example: Dave made a will leaving half his estate to his sister and the other half to be shared by his three children. He later has another child and does not revise his will. After his death his will could be revoked because the fourth child was omitted.

It is best to rewrite your will at the birth of a child. However, another solution is to include the following clause after the names of your children in your will.

…and any afterborn children living at the time of my death, in equal shares.

If you have one or more children and are leaving all of your property to your spouse, then your will would not be affected by the birth of a subsequent child.

YOUR DEBTS

One of the duties of the person administering an estate (called the *personal representative*) is to pay the debts of the decedent. Before an estate is distributed, the *legitimate* debts must be ascertained and paid. These debts include (but are not limited to) mortgages, car payments, and utilities.

An exception is *secured debts*, which are debts that are protected by a *lien* against property, such as a home loan or a car loan. In the case of a secured debt, the loan does not have to be paid before the property is distributed.

Example: John owns a $100,000 house with a $80,000 mortgage and he has $100,000 in the bank. If he leaves the house to his brother and the bank account to his sister, then his brother would receive the home but would owe the $80,000 mortgage.

What if your debts are more than your property? Today, unlike hundreds of years ago, people cannot inherit other peoples' debts. A person's property is used to pay their probate and funeral expenses first, and if there is not enough left to pay their other debts, then the creditors are out of luck. However, if a person leaves property to people and does not have enough assets to pay his or her debts, then the property will be sold to pay the debts.

Example: Jeb's will leaves all of his property to his three children. At the time of his death, Jeb, has $30,000 in medical bills, $11,000 in credit card debt, and his only assets are his car and $5,000 in stock. The car and stock would be sold and the funeral bill and probate fees paid out of the proceeds. If any money was left it would go to the creditors and nothing would be left for the children. The children would not have to pay the medical bills or credit card debt.

ESTATE AND INHERITANCE TAXES

Unlike some states, Georgia does not have estate or inheritance taxes in most cases. The only time estate taxes would be paid to the state of Georgia would be if the estate was subject to federal estate taxes and a credit was allowed for state taxes. Then these taxes would be paid to the state and credited against the federal tax due.

There is a federal estate tax for estates above a certain amount. Estates below that amount are allowed a *unified credit*, which exempts them from tax. The unified credit applies to the estate a person can leave at death and to gifts during his or her lifetime. In 2002, the amount exempted by the unified credit is $700,000 but it will rise to $1,000,000 by the year 2006. The amount will change according to the following schedule.

Year	Amount
2002-2003	$700,000
2004	$850,000
2005	$950,000
2006	$1,000,000

ANNUAL EXCLUSION

When a person makes a gift, that gift is subtracted from the amount entitled to the unified credit available to his or her estate at death. However, a person is allowed to make gifts of up to $10,000 per person per year without having these subtracted from the unified credit. This means a married couple can make gifts of up to $20,000 per year. The Taxpayer Relief Act of 1997 provided that this exclusion amount will be adjusted for inflation.

NEEDING A GEORGIA WILL 2

Any person who is fourteen years of age and of sound mind can make a valid will in Georgia. With that said, this chapter will describe what a will can and cannot do. It is important to know who is involved in this process, and whether wills from another state are valid in Georgia. This chapter covers this as well.

WHAT A WILL CAN DO

A will involves different people with different roles. Each one is affected by a will in specific ways.

BENEFICIARIES
A will allows you to decide who gets your property after your death. You can give specific personal items to certain persons and choose which of your friends or relatives, if any, deserve a greater share of your estate. You can also leave gifts to schools and charities. Anyone who gets property from a will is called a *beneficiary*. (*Heirs* are different from beneficiaries. Beneficiaries are named in the will, while heirs are those that get property if no beneficiaries are named (such as your children, grandchildren, parents, etc.) according to state laws.)

PERSONAL REPRESENTATIVE
A will allows you to decide who will be in charge of handling your estate. This is the person who gathers together all your assets and distributes them to the beneficiaries, hires attorneys or accountants if necessary, and files any essential tax or probate forms.

In Georgia, this person is called the *personal representative*. (In other states he or she may be called the *executor* or *executrix*.) With a will, you can provide that your personal representative does not have to post a *surety bond* with the court in order to serve and this can save your estate some money. (A surety bond is a financial guaranty issued by a bonding company to ensure that the personal representative performs as the law requires.) You can also give him or her the power to sell your property and take other actions without getting a court order.

GUARDIAN

A will allows you to choose a *guardian* for your minor children. This way you can avoid fights among relatives and make sure the best person raises your children. You may also appoint separate guardians over your children and over their money.

Example: You may appoint your sister as guardian over your children, and your father as guardian over their money. That way, a second person can keep an eye on how the children's money is being spent.

PROTECTING HEIRS

You can set up a trust to provide that your property is not distributed immediately. Many people feel that their children would not be ready to handle large sums of money at the *age of majority*. In most states this is eighteen, but in Georgia it is fourteen. A will can direct that the money is held until the children are twenty-one, or twenty-five, or older.

MINIMIZING TAXES

If your estate is over the amount protected by the federal *unified credit* (see page 9) then it will be subject to federal estate taxes. If you wish to lower those taxes, for example by making gifts to charities, you can do so through a will. However, such estate planning is beyond the scope of this book and you should consult an estate planning attorney or another book for further information.

DYING WITHOUT A WILL

If you do not have a will, Georgia law provides that your property shall be distributed as follows.

- If you leave a spouse and no children, your spouse gets your entire estate.

- If you leave a spouse and children they will each inherit an equal share but the spouses share shall not be less than one-third of the estate.

- If you leave no spouse, all of your children get equal shares of your estate.

- If you leave no spouse and no children then your estate would go to the highest persons on the following list who are living:

  - your parents;

  - your brothers and sisters, or if dead, their children;

  - your nieces and nephews;

  - your grandparents;

  - your uncles and aunts or their descendants; or

  - relatives of your deceased spouse.

OUT-OF-STATE WILLS

A will that is valid in another state would probably be valid to pass property in Georgia. However, if the will is not *self-proved*, a person in your former state would have to be appointed as a *Commissioner* to take the oath of a person who signed and witnessed your signature on the will before a Georgia Probate Court would accept it. Because of the expense and delay in having a Commissioner appointed and the problems in finding out-of-state witnesses, it is advisable to execute a new will after moving to Georgia.

Another advantage to having a Georgia will is that as a Georgia resident your estate will pay no state probate or inheritance taxes. If you move to Georgia but keep your old will, your former state of residence may try to collect taxes on your estate.

Georgia also allows a will to be *self-proved* so that the witnesses never have to be called in to take an oath. With special self-proving language in your will the witnesses take the oath at the time of signing and never have to be seen again.

Example: George and Barbara left their high-tax state and retired to Georgia, which has no estate or inheritance taxes, but they never made a new will. Upon their deaths their former state of residence tried to collect a tax from their estate because their old wills stated that they were residents of that state.

WHAT A WILL CANNOT DO

A will cannot direct that anything illegal be done and it cannot put unreasonable conditions on a gift. A provision that your daughter gets all of your property if she divorces her husband would be ignored by the court. She would get the property with no conditions attached. You can put some conditions in your will. For example, you may want to leave money to your brother only if he quits smoking, or to a hospital only if they name a wing in your honor. To be sure they are enforceable you should consult with an attorney.

A will cannot leave money or property to an animal because animals cannot legally own property. If you wish to continue paying for care of an animal after your death, you should leave the funds in trust or to a friend whom you know will care for the animal.

USING A SIMPLE WILL

The wills in this book will pass your property whether your estate is $1,000 or $100,000,000. However, if your estate is over $700,000 (this amount will rise to $1,000,000 by the year 2006) then you might be able to avoid estate taxes by using a trust or other tax-saving device. The larger your estate, the more you can save on estate taxes by doing more complicated planning. If you have a large estate and are concerned about estate taxes, you should consult an estate planning attorney or a book on estate planning.

WHO SHOULD NOT USE A SIMPLE WILL

There are certain situations where you may want to consult an attorney when writing your will.

WILL CONTEST

If you expect that there may be a fight over your estate or that someone might contest your will's validity, then you should consult a lawyer. If you leave less than the *statutory share* (amount required by law) of your estate to your spouse, or if you leave one or more of your children out of your will, it is likely that someone will contest your will.

COMPLICATED ESTATES

If you are the beneficiary of a trust or have any complications in your legal relationships, you may need special provisions in your will.

BLIND OR UNABLE TO WRITE

A person who is blind or who can sign only with an "X" should also consult a lawyer about the proper way to make and execute a will.

ESTATES OVER $700,000

If you expect to have over $700,000 (this amount will rise to $1,000,000 by the year 2006) at the time of your death, you may want to consult with a CPA or tax attorney regarding tax consequences.

Making a
Simple Will 3

Now that you know what a simple will is and what it can do, this chapter will break down the parts of a simple will. People that your will may affect will be described and specific will items will be discussed.

Parties in Your Will

As mentioned in Chapter 2, many different people can be affected by your will in specific ways.

PEOPLE   When making your will, it is important to clearly identify the persons you name as your beneficiaries. In some families, names differ only by middle initial or by Jr. or Sr. Be sure to check everyone's name before making your will. You can also add your relationship to the beneficiary, and their location such as "my cousin, John Xavier Doe of Peachtree City, Georgia."

ORGANIZATIONS   The same applies to organizations and charities as for people. There may be more than one group using the words "cancer society" or "heart association" in their name. Be sure to get the correct name of the group that you want to receive your gift.

SPOUSE AND   In most states, you must mention your spouse and children in your will
CHILDREN   even if you do not leave them any property. That is to show that you are of sound mind and know who your heirs are. As mentioned earlier, if you have a spouse or children and plan to leave your property to persons other than them, you should consult an attorney to be sure that your will will be enforceable.

PERSONAL PROPERTY

Because people acquire and dispose of *personal property* so often, it is not advisable to list a lot of small items in your will. Otherwise, when you sell or replace one of them you may have to rewrite your will.

One solution is to describe the type of item you wish to give.

Example: Instead of saying, "I leave my 1998 Ford to my sister," you should say, "I leave any automobile I own at the time of my death to my sister."

Of course, if you do mean to give a specific item you should describe it.

Example: Instead of "I leave my diamond ring to Joan," you should say, "I leave to Joan the one-half carat diamond ring that I inherited from my grandmother." You might own more than one diamond ring at the time of your death.

SPECIFIC BEQUESTS

Occasionally a person will want to leave a little something to a friend, charity, or the rest to the family. This can be done with a *specific bequest* such as "$1,000 to my dear friend Martha Jones." Of course there could be a problem if, at the time of a person's death, there was not anything left after the specific bequests.

Example: At the time of making his will, Todd had $1,000,000 in assets. He felt generous so he left $50,000 to a local hospital, $50,000 to a local group that took care of homeless animals and the rest to his children. Unfortunately, several years later, the stock market crashed and he committed suicide by jumping off a bridge. His estate at the time was worth only $110,000 so after the above specific bequests and the legal fees and expenses of probate, there was nothing left for his five children.

Another problem with specific bequests is that some of the property may be worth considerably more or less at death than when the will was made.

Example: Joe wanted his two children to equally share his estate. His will left his son his stocks (worth $500,000 at the time) and his daughter $500,000 in cash. By the time of Joe's death the stock was only worth $100,000.

He should have left "fifty percent" of his estate to each child. If giving certain things to certain people is an important part of your estate plan, you can give specific items to specific persons, but remember to make changes if your assets change.

JOINT
BENEFICIARIES

Be careful about leaving one item of personal property to more than one person.

Example: If you leave something to your son and his wife, what would happen if they divorce? Even if you leave something to two of your own children, what if they cannot agree about who will have possession of it? Whenever possible, leave property to one person.

REMAINDER CLAUSE

One of the most important clauses in a will is the *remainder clause*. This is the clause that says something like "all the rest of my property I leave to…" This clause makes sure that the will disposes of all property owned at the time of death and that nothing is forgotten.

In a simple will the best way to distribute property is to put it all in the remainder clause. In the example of Todd in the previous section on page 18, the problem would have been avoided if the will had read as follows: "The rest, residue, and remainder of my estate I leave, five percent to ABC Hospital, five percent to XYZ Animal Welfare League and ninety percent to be divided equally among my children…"

ALTERNATE BENEFICIARIES

You should always provide for an *alternate beneficiary* in case the person you name dies before you and you do not have a chance to make out a new will.

SURVIVOR OR
DESCENDANTS

Suppose your will leaves your property to your sister and brother but your brother predeceases you. Should his share go to your sister or to your brother's children or grandchildren?

If you are giving property to two or more persons and if you want it all to go to the other if one of them dies, then you would specify "or the survivor of them."

If, on the other hand, you want the property to go to the children of the deceased person you should state in your will, "or their lineal descendants." This would include his or her children and grandchildren.

FAMILY OR
PERSON

If you decide you want property to go to your brother's children and grandchildren, you must next decide if an equal share should go to each family or to each person.

Example: If your brother leaves three grandchildren, and one is an only child of his daughter and the others are the children of his son, should all grandchildren get equal shares, or should they take their parent's share?

When you want each family to get an equal share it is called *per stirpes*. When you want each person to get an equal share it is called *per capita*. Most of the wills in this book use per stirpes because that is the most common way property is left. If you wish to leave your property per capita then you can rewrite the will with this change.

Example: Alice leaves her property to her two daughters, Mary and Pat in equal shares, or to their lineal descendants per stirpes. Pat dies before Alice, leaving two children. In this case Mary would get half of the estate and Pat's children would split the other half of the estate. If Alice had specified per capita instead of per stirpes then Mary, and Pat's two children would have each gotten one-third of the estate.

Per Stirpes Distribution

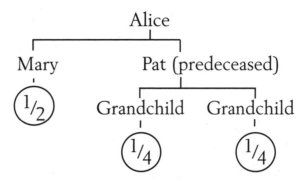

Per Capita Distribution

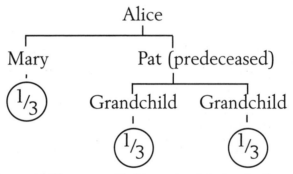

There are fourteen different will forms in this book that should cover the options most people want, but you may want to divide your property slightly differently from what is stated in these forms. If so, you can retype the forms according to these rules, specifying whether the property should go to the survivor or the lineal descendants. If this is confusing to you, you should consider seeking the advice of an attorney.

SURVIVORSHIP

Many people put a clause in their will stating that anyone receiving property under the will must survive for thirty days (or forty-five or sixty) after the death of the person who made the will. This is so that if the two people die in the same accident there will not be two probates and the property will not go to the other party's heirs.

Example: Fred and Wilma were married and each had children by previous marriages. They did not have survivorship clauses in their wills and they were in an airplane crash and died. Fred's children hired several expert witnesses and a large law firm to prove that at the time of the crash Fred lived for a few minutes longer than Wilma. That way, when Wilma died first, all of her property went to Fred. When he died a few minutes later, all of Fred *and* Wilma's property went to his children. Wilma's children got nothing.

GUARDIANS

If you have minor children you should name a guardian for them. There are two types of guardians, a guardian over the *person* and a guardian over the *property*. The first is the person who decides where the children will live and makes the other parental decisions for them. A guardian of the property is in charge of the minor's property and inheritance. In most cases, one person is appointed guardian of both the person and property. But some people prefer the children to live with one person, but to have the money held by another person.

Example: Sandra was a widow with a young daughter. She knew that if anything happened to her, her sister would be the best person to raise her daughter. But her sister was never good with money. So when Sandra made out her will, she named her sister as guardian over the person of her daughter and she named her father as guardian over the estate of her daughter.

NOTE: *When naming a guardian, it is always advisable to name an alternate guardian in case your first choice is unable to serve for any reason.*

CHILDREN'S TRUST

When a parent dies leaving a minor child and the child's property is held by a guardian, the guardianship ends when the child reaches the age of eighteen, and all of the property is turned over to the child. Most parents do not feel their children are competent at the age of eighteen to handle large sums of money and prefer that it be held until the child is twenty-one, twenty-five, thirty, or even older.

If you wish to set up a complicated system of determining when your children should receive various amounts of your estate, or if you want the property held to a higher age than thirty-five, you should consult a lawyer to draft a trust. However, if you want a simple provision that the funds be held until they reach a higher age than eighteen, and you have someone you trust to make decisions about paying for education or other expenses for your child or children, you can put that provision in your will as a children's trust.

The children's trust trustee can be the same person as the guardian, or it can be a different person. It is advisable to name an alternate trustee in case your first choice is unable to handle it.

PERSONAL REPRESENTATIVE

A *personal representative* is the person who will be in charge of your probate. He or she will:

- gather your assets;
- handle the sale of your assets if necessary;
- prepare an inventory;
- hire an attorney; and
- distribute the property.

This should be a person you trust, and if it is, then you can state in your will that no bond will be required to be posted by him or her. Otherwise the court will require that a surety bond be paid for by your estate to guarantee that the person is honest. You can appoint a bank to handle your estate, but their fees are usually very high.

It is best to appoint a Georgia resident, both because it is easier and because a bond may be required of a non-resident even if your will waives it.

MULTIPLE APPOINTEES

Some people like to name two persons to handle their estate to avoid jealousy, or to have them check on each other's honesty. However, this is not a good idea. It makes double work in getting the papers signed, and there can be problems if they cannot agree on something.

FEES

The person handling your estate is usually entitled to compensation. A family member will often waive the fee. If there is a lot of work involved he or she may request the fee, or other family members may insist that he or she take one. You can insist in your will that your personal representative is paid a fee.

WITNESSES

In Georgia a will must be witnessed by two persons to be valid. In all other states two witnesses are required, except Vermont which requires three. So unless you own property in Vermont, you only need to have two witnesses.

The witnesses should not be people who are beneficiaries of your will. While it does not invalidate your whole will, it makes the gifts to that witness void.

SELF-PROVING AFFIDAVIT

A will only needs two witnesses to be legal, but if you also have it *notarized* it will make the process of probating the will much simpler. If a will is not notarized, then at the time of your death one of the witnesses must sign a paper attesting to the validity of your will. With the notary your will is admitted to probate without delay.

To properly notarize a will you must use a SELF-PROVED WILL AFFIDAVIT. This is included in Appendix B. (see form 17, p.93.)

SELF-PROVING WILL PROTECTION FORM

One additional step you can take to protect your will is to make a copy of it and attach a SELF-PROVING WILL PROTECTION FORM to it. This way if your original will is lost or destroyed your copy can be probated. This form is included in Appendix B. (see form 19, p.97.)

There is one danger in using this form. If you intend to destroy your will and make a new will you must also remember to destroy the copy or it may be probated.

DISINHERITING SOMEONE

Because it may result in your will being challenged in court, you should not make your own will if you intend to disinherit someone. However, you may wish to leave one child less than another because you already made a gift to that child, or perhaps because that child needs the money less than the other.

If you do give more to one child than to another, then you should state your reasons to show that you thought out your plan. Otherwise the one who received less might argue that you did not realize what you were doing and were not competent to make a will.

FUNERAL ARRANGEMENTS

There is no harm in stating your preferences in your will, but in most states, directions for a funeral are not legally enforceable. Often a will is not found until after the funeral. Therefore it is better to tell your family about your wishes or to make prior arrangements yourself.

HANDWRITTEN WILLS

In some states a person can hand write a will, without any witnesses, and it will be held valid. This is called a *holographic* will. In Georgia, a handwritten or holographic will is not valid.

FORMS

There are fourteen different will forms included in this book for easy use. You can either tear them out, photocopy them, or retype them on plain paper.

The forms in this book are printed on both sides of the page. If you photocopy them on separate pages or type your will on more than one piece of paper you should staple the pages together, initial each page and have both witnesses initial each page. Each page should state at the bottom, "page 1 of 3," "page 2 of 3," etc.

CORRECTIONS

Your will should have no white-outs or erasures. If for some reason it is impossible to make a will without corrections, the corrections should be initialed by you and both witnesses.

EXECUTING YOUR WILL 4

The signing of a will is a serious legal event and must be done properly or the will may be declared invalid. Preferably, it should be done in a private room without distraction. All parties must watch each other sign and no one should leave the scene until all have signed.

Example: Ebenezer was bedridden in a small room. His will was brought in to him to sign, but the witnesses could not actually see his hand signing because a dresser was in the way. His will was ignored by the court and his property went to two persons who were not in his will.

PROCEDURE

To be sure your will is valid, you should follow these rules:

- You must state to your witnesses: "This is my will. I have read it and I understand it and this is how I want it to read. I want you two (or three) people to be my witnesses." Contrary to popular belief, you do not have to read it to the witnesses or to let them read it.

- You must date your will and sign your name at the end in ink exactly as it is printed in the will, and you should initial each page as both witnesses watch.

- You and the other witnesses must watch as each witness signs in ink and initials each page.

SELF-PROVED WILL AFFIDAVIT

A will only needs two witnesses to be legal, but if you also have it notarized, it will make the process of probating the will much simpler. If a will is not notarized, then at the time of your death one of the witnesses must sign a paper attesting to the validity of your will. With the notary, your will is admitted to probate without delay.

To properly notarize a will you must use a SELF-PROVED WILL AFFIDAVIT. This is included in Appendix B. (see form 17, p.93.)

SELF-PROVING WILL PROTECTION FORM

If you wish to have a second valid copy of your will, you can make a photocopy and execute a SELF-PROVING WILL PROTECTION FORM. (see form 19, p.97.) This needs to be signed by you and the witnesses and notarized.

NOTE: *If you intend to destroy your will and make a new will, you must remember to also destroy the copy or it may be probated.*

AFTER SIGNING YOUR WILL 5

Properly signing your will does not end your responsibility. You must ensure its safe keeping so it can be found and executed at your death.

PROTECTING AND STORING YOUR WILL

By now you know just how important and valuable your will is to ensure that your instructions for the distribution of your property and other matters are carried out as you wish after your death.

If your will is lost or destroyed, then the court will presume that you intended to revoke your will. This then forces your heirs to prove that you did not revoke your will.

In many cases this legal presumption has caused a great deal of hardship as it has proved virtually impossible for some families—particularly those of limited means or abilities—to overcome the presumption of intended revocation invoked by the court when a will is lost or destroyed. Many families have suffered when the final wishes of the decedent were replaced by court-imposed distributions.

Protecting your family and loved ones is not difficult if you follow these simple steps:

1. Store the copy of your will separately from the original will and safeguard it as you would the original. It can be used in place of the original if the original is lost.

2. Never doodle or in any way mutilate either the original or the copy of the will as it may be decided that you were attempting to destroy your will.

3. Select a secure place for your original will and the copy that will provide protection from theft, fire or other loss. Most of all, remember, do not store the original and the copy in the same place.

   Your personal representative should always know the whereabouts of your will and it should be easily accessible to your heirs.

   If you are hesitant or concerned about the contents of your will being known before your death, there is no duty or obligation on your part to tell anyone about the contents and your will is not filed anywhere until after your death. No one has to know what is in your will while you are alive.

   A good strategy might be to place the original in the hands of your attorney and the copy in a safe deposit box in your bank. In the State of Georgia, after your death it is easy for your representative or attorney to get your will out of a safe deposit box.

   If you prefer to rely on your own devices as to where you store the copy, please remember that you should use a locked safe or fire proof box in your home or some other safe place that you control and are comfortable using.

4. Review your will periodically. If you change your will, remember to make *a new copy of the new will* following the suggestions in this book and then **destroy the old will and the copy of the old will**. Then make out a new SELF-PROVING WILL PROTECTION FORM and attach it to the new copy before placing the will and copy in safekeeping. (see form 19, p.97.)

REVOKING YOUR WILL

The usual way to revoke a will is to execute a new one that states that it revokes all previously made wills. To revoke a will without making a new one, one can tear, burn, cancel, deface, obliterate, or destroy it, as long as this is done with the intention of revoking it. If this is done accidentally, the will is not legally revoked.

Example: Ralph tells his son Clyde to go to the basement safe and tear up his (Ralph's) will. If Clyde does not tear it up in Ralph's presence, it is probably not effectively revoked.

REVIVAL   What if you change your will by drafting a new one, and later decide you do not like the changes and want to go back to your old will? Can you destroy the new one and revive the old one? *No!* Once you execute a new will revoking an old will, you cannot revive the old will unless you execute a new document stating that you intend to revive the old will. In other words, you really should execute a new will.

CHANGING YOUR WILL

You should not make any changes on your will after it has been signed. If you cross out a person's name or add a clause to a will that has already been signed, your change will not be valid and your entire will might become invalid.

One way to amend a will is to execute a *codicil*. A CODICIL TO WILL is an amendment to a will. (see form 18, p.95.) However, a CODICIL TO WILL must be executed just like a will. It must have the same number of witnesses, and to be self-proved it must include a self-proving page that must be notarized. (see form 17, p.93.)

Because a CODICIL TO WILL requires the same formality as a will, it is usually better to just make a new will.

In an emergency situation, if you want to change something in your will, but cannot get to a notary to have it self-proved, you can execute a CODICIL TO WILL, which is witnessed, but not self-proved. As long as it is properly witnessed (two witnesses) it will legally change your will. The only drawback would be that the witnesses would have to later sign an oath if it was not self-proved.

Use form 18 to prepare a CODICIL TO WILL and form 17 to self-prove the codicil.

MAKING A LIVING WILL 6

A LIVING WILL is not a videotape of a person making a will. It has nothing to do with the usual type of will that distributes property. A LIVING WILL is a document by which a person declares that he or she does not want artificial life support systems used if he or she becomes terminally ill.

Modern science can often keep a body alive even if the brain is permanently dead, or if the person is in constant pain. In recent years, all states have legalized living wills either by statute or by court decision.

The state of Georgia does not have a specific form to be used as a LIVING WILL. Any writing that clearly expresses the wishes of the person signing it, which is signed in front of two witnesses who are not blood relatives or a spouse, can be used.

If the person is physically unable to sign, he or she may read the LIVING WILL out loud and direct one of the witnesses to sign it for him or her.

The form included as a LIVING WILL in Appendix B is from the Georgia Statutes. (see form 20, p.99.) It can be taken out of this book and used, photocopied, retyped, or rewritten by hand.

MAKING ANATOMICAL GIFTS 7

Since 1969, Georgia has allowed its residents who are eighteen years of age or older and of sound mind to donate their bodies or organs for research or transplantation. Consent may be given by a relative of a deceased person, but because relatives are often in shock or too upset to make such a decision, it is better to have one's intent made clear before death. This can be done by a statement in a will or by another signed document such as a UNIFORM DONOR CARD. (see form 21, p.101.) The gift may be of all or part of one's body, and it may be made to a specific person such as a physician or an ill relative.

The document making the donation must be signed before two witnesses who must also sign in each other's presence. If the donor cannot sign, then the document may be signed for him or her at his or her direction in the presence of the witnesses.

The donor may designate in the document who the physician is that will carry out the procedure.

If the document or will has been delivered to a specific donee it may be amended or revoked by the donor in the following ways:

- by executing and delivering a signed statement to the donee;

- by an oral statement to two witnesses communicated to the donee;

- by an oral statement during a terminal illness made to an attending physician and communicated to the donee; or

- by a signed document found on the person of the donor or in his or her effects.

If a document of a gift has not been delivered to a donee, then it may be revoked by any of the above methods or by destruction, cancellation, or mutilation of the document. It may also be revoked in the same method a will is revoked as described on page 31.

A Uniform Donor Card is included in Appendix B. (see form 21, p.101.) It must be signed in the presence of two signing witnesses.

If you wish to have more specific information included relating to an organ donation, or relating to any will matter, contact an attorney.

GLOSSARY

A

administrator (*administratrix* if female). A person appointed by the court to oversee distribution of the property of someone who died (either without a will, or if the person designated in the will is unable to serve).

attested will. A will which includes an attestation clause and has been signed in front of witnesses.

B

beneficiary. A person who is entitled to receive property from a person who died (regardless of whether there is a will).

bequest. Personal property left to someone in a will.

C

children's trust. A trust set up to hold property given to children. Usually it provides that the children will not receive their property until they reach a higher age than the age of majority.

codicil. An amendment to a will.

community property. Property acquired by a husband and wife by their labors during their marriage.

D

decedent. A person who has died.

descendent. A child, grandchild, great-grandchild, etc.

devise. Real property left to someone in a will. A person who is entitled to a devise is called a *devisee*.

donee. Person or organization that receives the benefit of a gift.

E

elective share. In non-community property states, the portion of the estate which may be taken by a surviving spouse, regardless of what the will says.

estate. All of the property and debts owned by a person.

executor (*executrix* if female). A person appointed in a will to oversee distribution of the property of someone who died with a will. However, in Georgia today, this person is called a *personal representative*.

exempt property. Property that is exempt from distribution as a normal part of the estate.

F

family allowance. An amount of money set aside from the estate to support the family of the decedent for a period of time.

forced share. *See* **elective share**.

H

heir. A person who will inherit from a decedent who died without a will.

holographic will. A will in which all of the material provisions are entirely in the handwriting of the maker. Holographic wills are not legal in Georgia.

I

intestate. Without making a will. One who dies without a will is said to have *died intestate*.

intestate share. In non-community property states, the portion of the estate a spouse is entitled to receive if there is no will.

J

joint tenancy. A type of property ownership by two or more persons, in which if one owner dies, that owner's interest goes to the other joint tenants (not to the deceased owner's heirs as in tenancy in common).

L

legacy. Real property left to someone in a will. A person who is entitled to a legacy is called a *legatee*.

living will. A document expressing the writer's desires regarding how medical care is to be handled in the event the writer is not able to express his or her wishes concerning the use of life-prolonging medical procedures.

P

per capita. Distribution of property with equal shares going to each person.

per stirpes. Distribution of property with equal shares going to each family line.

personal representative. A person appointed by the court, or will, to oversee distribution of the property of the person who died. This is a more modern term than "administrator," "executor," etc., and applies regardless of whether there is a will.

probate. The process of settling a decedent's estate through the probate court.

R

residue. The property that is left over in an estate after all specific bequests and devises.

S

self-proving affidavit. A form added to a will in which the will maker and witnesses state under oath that they have signed and witnessed the will.

specific bequest *or* **specific devise**. A gift in a will of a specific item of property, or a specific amount of cash.

statutory will. A will which has been prepared according to the requirements of a statute.

T

tenancy by the entirety. A type of property ownership by a married couple, in which the property automatically passes to one spouse upon the death of the other. This is basically the same as joint tenancy, except that it is only between a husband and wife.

tenancy in common. Ownership of property by two or more people, in which each owner's share would descend to that owner's heirs (not to the other owners as in joint tenancy).

testate. With a will. One who dies with a will is said to have *died testate*.

testator. (*testatrix* if female.) A person who makes his or her will.

Totten trust. Assets that are titled in the name of the owner, in trust for another person. The owner controls the assets while still alive. The one in trust becomes the new owner when the old owner dies.

W

will. A document that distributes all of a person's property after he or she dies.

APPENDIX A
SAMPLE FILLED-IN FORMS

The following pages include sample filled-in forms for some of the wills in this book. They are filled out in different ways for different situations. You should look at all of them to see how the different sections can be filled in. Only one example of a SELF-PROVED WILL AFFIDAVIT is shown, but you should use it with every will. (see form 17, p.50.)

Last Will and Testament

I, _____John Smith_____ a resident of _____Cherokee_____
County, Georgia do hereby make, publish, and declare this to be my Last Will and Testament, hereby revoking any and all Wills and Codicils heretofore made by me.

FIRST: I direct that all my just debts and funeral expenses be paid out of my estate as soon after my death as is practicable.

SECOND: I give, devise, and bequeath the following specific gifts:
Chip Smith, my sixteen souvenir silver spoons;------------------------------
Jo Anne Smith, my Liberace LP set;--
Reginald Smith, my golf clubs.--

THIRD: I give, devise, and bequeath all my estate, real, personal, and mixed, of whatever kind and wherever situated, of which I may die seized or possessed, or in which I may have any interest or over which I may have any power of appointment or testamentary disposition, to my spouse, _____Barbara Smith_____. If my said spouse does not survive me, I give, and bequeath the said property to my sisters, Jan Smith, Joan Smith, and Jennifer Smith in equal shares-------------------------------
--,
or the survivor of them.

FOURTH: In the event that any beneficiary fails to survive me by thirty days, then this will shall take effect as if that person had predeceased me.

FIFTH: I hereby nominate, constitute, and appoint _____Barbara Smith_____
as Personal Representative of this, my Last Will and Testament. In the event that such named person is unable or unwilling to serve at any time or for any reason, then I nominate, constitute, and appoint _____Reginald Smith_____ as Personal Representative in the place and stead of the person first named herein. It is my will and I direct that my Personal Representative shall not be required to furnish a bond for the faithful performance of his or her duties in any jurisdiction, any provision of law to the contrary notwithstanding, and I give my Personal Representative full power to administer my estate, including the power to settle claims, pay debts, and sell, lease or exchange real and personal property without court order.

IN WITNESS WHEREOF I declare this to be my Last Will and Testament and execute it willingly as my free and voluntary act for the purposes expressed herein and I am of legal age and sound mind and make this under no constraint or undue influence, this _29th_ day of _January_, 2002 at _____Cherokee_____ State of _____Georgia_____.

Initials: __*J.S.*__ __*B.J.*__ __*J.D.*__   Page _1_ of _3_
         Testator   Witness   Witness

John Smith   L.S.

The foregoing instrument was on said date subscribed at the end thereof by John Smith , the above named Testator who signed, published, and declared this instrument to be his/her Last Will and Testament in the presence of us and each of us, who thereupon at his/her request, in his/her presence, and in the presence of each other, have hereunto subscribed our names as witnesses thereto. We are of sound mind and proper age to witness a will and understand this to be his/her will, and to the best of our knowledge testator is of legal age to make a will, of sound mind, and under no constraint or undue influence.

Brenda Jones residing at Marietta, Georgia

John Doe residing at Atlanta, Georgia

NOTE: _The **SELF-PROVED WILL AFFIDAVIT** (form 17) would appear as page 3 (or the last page) of the will._

Last Will and Testament

I, _____John Smith_____ a resident of _____Cherokee_____ County, Georgia do hereby make, publish, and declare this to be my Last Will and Testament, hereby revoking any and all Wills and Codicils heretofore made by me.

FIRST: I direct that all my just debts and funeral expenses be paid out of my estate as soon after my death as is practicable.

SECOND: I give, devise, and bequeath the following specific gifts:
Stella Smith, my five George Eliot literary works book collection; -----------
Richard Jones, my antique bedwarmer. --

THIRD: I give, devise, and bequeath all my estate, real, personal, and mixed, of whatever kind and wherever situated, of which I may die seized or possessed, or in which I may have any interest or over which I may have any power of appointment or testamentary disposition, to my spouse, _____Barbara Smith_____. If my said spouse does not survive me, I give, and bequeath the said property to my children _Amy Smith,_ _Beamy Smith, and Seamy Smith---_ _--,_ in equal shares or to their lineal descendants, per stirpes.

FOURTH: In the event that any beneficiary fails to survive me by thirty days, then this will shall take effect as if that person had predeceased me.

FIFTH: I hereby nominate, constitute, and appoint _____Barbara Smith_____ as Personal Representative of this, my Last Will and Testament. In the event that such named person is unable or unwilling to serve at any time or for any reason, then I nominate, constitute, and appoint _____Reginald Smith_____ as Personal Representative in the place and stead of the person first named herein. It is my will and I direct that my Personal Representative shall not be required to furnish a bond for the faithful performance of his or her duties in any jurisdiction, any provision of law to the contrary notwithstanding, and I give my Personal Representative full power to administer my estate, including the power to settle claims, pay debts, and sell, lease or exchange real and personal property without court order.

IN WITNESS WHEREOF I declare this to be my Last Will and Testament and execute it willingly as my free and voluntary act for the purposes expressed herein and I am of legal age and sound mind and make this under no constraint or undue influence, this _5th_ day of _January_, 2002 at _·Cherokee_ State of _Georgia_.

Initials:	**J.S.**	**B.J.**	**J.D.**	Page _1_ of _3_
	Testator	Witness	Witness	

<u>*John Smith*</u>   L.S.

     The foregoing instrument was on said date subscribed at the end thereof by <u>John Smith</u>, the above named Testator who signed, published, and declared this instrument to be his/her Last Will and Testament in the presence of us and each of us, who thereupon at his/her request, in his/her presence, and in the presence of each other, have hereunto subscribed our names as witnesses thereto. We are of sound mind and proper age to witness a will and understand this to be his/her will, and to the best of our knowledge testator is of legal age to make a will, of sound mind, and under no constraint or undue influence.

Barbara Jones _____ residing at <u>Atlanta, Georgia</u>

John Doe _____ residing at <u>Peaches, Georgia</u>

NOTE: *The **SELF-PROVED WILL AFFIDAVIT** (form 17) would appear as page 3 (or the last page) of the will.*

Last Will and Testament

I, _____John Doe_____ a resident of ___Peach___ County, Georgia do hereby make, publish, and declare this to be my Last Will and Testament, hereby revoking any and all Wills and Codicils heretofore made by me.

FIRST: I direct that all my just debts and funeral expenses be paid out of my estate as soon after my death as is practicable.

SECOND: I give, devise, and bequeath the following specific gifts:
Jane Doe, the Doe/Mayfield family portraits; ---------------------------------
Eileen Doe-Rogers, Grandpa's antique peg leg; ----------------------------------
Ralph Rogers, my gas-grill. --

THIRD: I give, devise, and bequeath all my estate, real, personal, and mixed, of whatever kind and wherever situated, of which I may die seized or possessed, or in which I may have any interest or over which I may have any power of appointment or testamentary disposition, to my children ___James Doe, Mary Doe, Larry Doe, Barry Doe, Carrie Doe, and Moe Doe___ --, plus any afterborn or adopted children in equal shares or to their lineal descendants per stirpes.

FOURTH: In the event that any beneficiary fails to survive me by thirty days, then this will shall take effect as if that person had predeceased me.

FIFTH: In the event any of my children have not attained the age of 18 years at the time of my death, I hereby nominate, constitute, and appoint ___Herbert Doe___ as guardian over the person of any of my children who have not reached the age of majority at the time of my death. In the event that said guardian is unable or unwilling to serve, then I nominate, constitute, and appoint ___Tom Doe___ as guardian. Said guardian shall serve without bond or surety.

SIXTH: In the event any of my children have not attained the age of 18 years at the time of my death, I hereby nominate, constitute, and appoint ___Herbert Doe___ as guardian over the property of any of my children who have not reached the age of majority at the time of my death. In the event that said guardian is unable or unwilling to serve, then I nominate, constitute, and appoint ___Tom Doe___ as guardian. Said guardian shall serve without bond or surety.

SEVENTH: I hereby nominate, constitute, and appoint ___Clarence Doe___ as Personal Representative of this, my Last Will and Testament. In the event that such named person is unable or unwilling to serve at any time or for any reason, then I nominate, consti-

Initials: __*J.D.*__ __*B.J.*__ __*J.D.*__   Page __1__ of __3__
Testator   Witness   Witness

tute, and appoint _____Englebert Doe_____ as Personal Representative in the place and stead of the person first named herein. It is my will and I direct that my Personal Representative shall not be required to furnish a bond for the faithful performance of his or her duties in any jurisdiction, any provision of law to the contrary notwithstanding, and I give my Personal Representative full power to administer my estate, including the power to settle claims, pay debts, and sell, lease or exchange real and personal property without court order.

IN WITNESS WHEREOF I declare this to be my Last Will and Testament and execute it willingly as my free and voluntary act for the purposes expressed herein and I am of legal age and sound mind and make this under no constraint or undue influence, this 11th day of ___March___, 2002 at ___Peach Tree___ State of ___Georgia___.

_____*John Doe*_____ L.S.

The foregoing instrument was on said date subscribed at the end thereof by _____John Doe_____, the above named Testator who signed, published, and declared this instrument to be his/her Last Will and Testament in the presence of us and each of us, who thereupon at his/her request, in his/her presence, and in the presence of each other, have hereunto subscribed our names as witnesses thereto. We are of sound mind and proper age to witness a will and understand this to be his/her will, and to the best of our knowledge testator is of legal age to make a will, of sound mind, and under no constraint or undue influence.

_____*Barbara Jones*_____residing at_Atlanta, Georgia_____

_____*John Dorian*_____residing at_Peaches, Georgia_____

Page _2_ of _3_

NOTE: *The **Self-Proved Will Affidavit** (form 17) would appear as page 3 (or the last page) of the will.*

Last Will and Testament

I, _____Mary Smith_____ a resident of ___Levy___
County, Georgia do hereby make, publish, and declare this to be my Last Will and Testament,
hereby revoking any and all Wills and Codicils heretofore made by me.

FIRST: I direct that all my just debts and funeral expenses be paid out of my estate as
soon after my death as is practicable.

SECOND: I give, devise, and bequeath the following specific gifts:
Rebecca Smith, my six Coco Chanel leather purses; --------------------------
Petunia Smith, my 4 carat smoky topaz and 1/8 carat diamond ring.-----------

THIRD: I give, devise, and bequeath all my estate, real, personal, and mixed, of whatever kind and wherever situated, of which I may die seized or possessed, or in which I may
have any interest or over which I may have any power of appointment or testamentary disposition, to the following:___my brothers John Smith and James Smith -------------
----
---,
or to the survivor of them.

FOURTH: In the event that any beneficiary fails to survive me by thirty days, then
this will shall take effect as if that person had predeceased me.

FIFTH: I hereby nominate, constitute, and appoint _____Herbert Doe_____ as
Personal Representative of this, my Last Will and Testament. In the event that such named
person is unable or unwilling to serve at any time or for any reason, then I nominate, constitute, and appoint _____Tom Doe_____ as Personal Representative in the
place and stead of the person first named herein. It is my will and I direct that my Personal
Representative shall not be required to furnish a bond for the faithful performance of his or
her duties in any jurisdiction, any provision of law to the contrary notwithstanding, and I give
my Personal Representative full power to administer my estate, including the power to settle claims, pay debts, and sell, lease or exchange real and personal property without court
order.

IN WITNESS WHEREOF I declare this to be my Last Will and Testament and execute it willingly as my free and voluntary act for the purposes expressed herein and I am of
legal age and sound mind and make this under no constraint or undue influence, this _6th_
day of _May_____, _2002_ at _____Chiefland_ State of _____Georgia_____.

_____*Mary Smith*_____ L.S.

Initials: __**M.S.**__ __**B.J.**__ __**J.D.**__   Page _1_ of _3_
   Testator   Witness   Witness

The foregoing instrument was on said date subscribed at the end thereof by

_____Mary Smith_____, the above named Testator who signed, published, and declared this instrument to be his/her Last Will and Testament in the presence of us and each of us, who thereupon at his/her request, in his/her presence, and in the presence of each other, have hereunto subscribed our names as witnesses thereto. We are of sound mind and proper age to witness a will and understand this to be his/her will, and to the best of our knowledge testator is of legal age to make a will, of sound mind, and under no constraint or undue influence.

_Barbara Jones______residing at___Atlanta, Georgia_____

_John Doe______residing at___Peaches, Georgia_____

Page __2__ of __3__

NOTE: *The **Self-Proved Will Affidavit** (form 17) would appear as page 3 (or the last page) of the will.*

Self-Proved Will Affidavit
(attach to Will)

STATE OF GEORGIA

COUNTY OF _____Peach_____

I, the undersigned, an officer authorized to administer oaths, certify that
_____John Doe_____, the testator and
____Jane Roe_____, and _____Melvin Coe_____,
the witnesses, whose names are signed to the attached or foregoing instrument and whose
signatures appear below, having appeared before me and having been first been duly sworn,
each then declared to me that: 1) the attached or foregoing instrument is the last will of the
testator; 2) the testator willingly and voluntarily declared, signed, and executed the will in
the presence of the witnesses; 3) the witnesses signed the will upon the request of the testator, in the presence and hearing of the testator and in the presence of each other; 4) to the
best knowledge of each witness, the testator was, at the time of signing, of the age of majority (or otherwise legally competent to make a will), of sound mind and memory, and under
no constraint or undue influence; and 5) each witness was and is competent and of proper
age to witness a will.

John Doe
_____ (Testator)

Jane Roe
_____ (Witness)

Melvin Coe
_____ (Witness)

Subscribed and sworn to before me by _____John Doe_____, the testator, who is personally known to me or who has produced GA driver's license_____
as identification, and by _____Jane Roe_____, a witness, who is personally known to me or who has produced ____GA driver's license_____ as identification, and by _____Melvin Coe_____, a witness, who is personally
known to me or who has produced ____GA driver's license_____ as identification, this
__5th__ day of_____July_____, _2002_.

C.U. Sine
_____
Notary or other officer

Codicil to the Will of

_____Larry Lowe_____

I, _____Larry Lowe_____, a resident of _____Leon_____ County, Georgia declare this to be the first codicil to my Last Will and Testament dated _____July 5_____, __2001__.

FIRST: I hereby revoke the clause of my Will which reads as follows: FOURTH: I hereby leave $5000.00 to my daughter Mildred.--------------------
----

---.

SECOND: I hereby add the following clause to my Will: FOURTH: I hereby leave $1000.00 to my daughter Mildred.--
----

---.

THIRD: In all other respects I hereby confirm and republish my Last Will and Testament dated _____July 5_____, ___2001___.

IN WITNESS WHEREOF, I have signed, published, and declared the foregoing instrument as and for a codicil to my Last Will and Testament, this ___5th___ day of _____January_____, __2002__.

_____*Larry Lowe*_____

The foregoing instrument was on the 5th day of _____January_____, 2002, signed at the end thereof, and at the same time published and declared by _____Larry Lowe_____, as and for a codicil to his/her Last Will and Testament, dated _____July 5_____, ___2001___, in the presence of each of us, who, this attestation clause having been read to us, did at the request of the said testator/testatrix, in his/her presence and in the presence of each other signed our names as witnesses thereto.

*James Smith*_____residing at_____Woodstock, Georgia_____

*Mary Smith*_____residing at_____Ila, Georgia_____

Living Will

Living will made this <u>29</u> day of <u>January, 2002</u> (month, year).

I, <u>Norman Milquetoast</u>, being of sound mind, willfully and voluntarily make known my desire that my life shall not be prolonged under the circumstances set forth below and do declare:

1. If at any time I should (check each option desired):

   (x) have a terminal condition,

   ( ) become in a coma with no reasonable expectation of regaining consciousness, or

   (x) become in a persistent vegetative state with no reasonable expectation of regaining significant cognitive function, as defined in and established in accordance with the procedures set forth in paragraphs (2), (9), and (13) of Code Section 31-32-2 of the Official Code of Georgia Annotated, I direct that the application of life-sustaining procedures to my body (check the option desired):

   (x) including nourishment and hydration,

   ( ) including nourishment but not hydration, or

   ( ) excluding nourishment and hydration, be withheld or withdrawn and that I be permitted to die;

2. In the absence of my ability to give directions regarding the use of such life-sustaining procedures, it is my intention that this living will shall be honored by my family and physician(s) as the final expression of my legal right to refuse medical or surgical treatment and accept the consequences from such refusal;

3. I understand that I may revoke this living will at any time;

4. I understand the full import of this living will, and I am at least 18 years of age and am emotionally and mentally competent to make this living will; and

5. If I am a female and I have been diagnosed as pregnant, this living will shall have no force and effect unless the fetus is not viable and I indicate by initialing after this sentence that I want this living will to be carried out._____(Initial)

Signed <u>**Norman Milquetoast**</u>

<u>Winter Haven</u> (City), <u>Peach</u> (County), and <u>Georgia</u> (State of Residence).

I hereby witness this living will and attest that:

(1) The declarant is personally known to me and I believe the declarant to be at least 18 years of age and of sound mind;

(2) I am at least 18 years of age;

(3) To the best of my knowledge, at the time of the execution of this living will, I:

    (A) Am not related to the declarant by blood or marriage;

    (B) Would not be entitled to any portion of the declarant's estate by any will or by operation of law under the rules of descent and distribution of this state;

    (C) Am not the attending physician of declarant or an employee of the attending physician or an employee of the hospital or skilled nursing facility in which declarant is a patient;

    (D) Am not directly financially responsible for the declarant's medical care; and

    (E) Have no present claim against any portion of the estate of the declarant;

(4) Declarant has signed this document in my presence as above instructed, on the date above first shown.

Witness   Harvey Nabor

Address   1236 Georgia Avenue

           Winter Haven, GA 33210

Witness   June Nabor

Address   1236 Georgia Avenue

           Winter Haven, GA 33210

Additional witness required when living will is signed in a hospital or skilled nursing facility.

I hereby witness this living will and attest that I believe the declarant to be of sound mind and to have made this living will willingly and voluntarily.

Witness:_____

Medical director of skilled nursing facility or staff physician not participating in care of the patient or chief of the hospital medical staff or staff physician or hospital designee not participating in care of the patient.

APPENDIX B
BLANK FORMS

The following pages contain forms that can be used to prepare a will, codicil, living will, and Uniform Donor Card. They should only be used by persons who have read this book, who do not have any complications in their legal affairs, and who understand the forms they are using. The forms may be used right out of the book or they may be photocopied or retyped.

How to Pick the Right Will

Follow the chart and use the form number in the black circle, then use form 17, the SELF-PROVED WILL AFFIDAVIT.

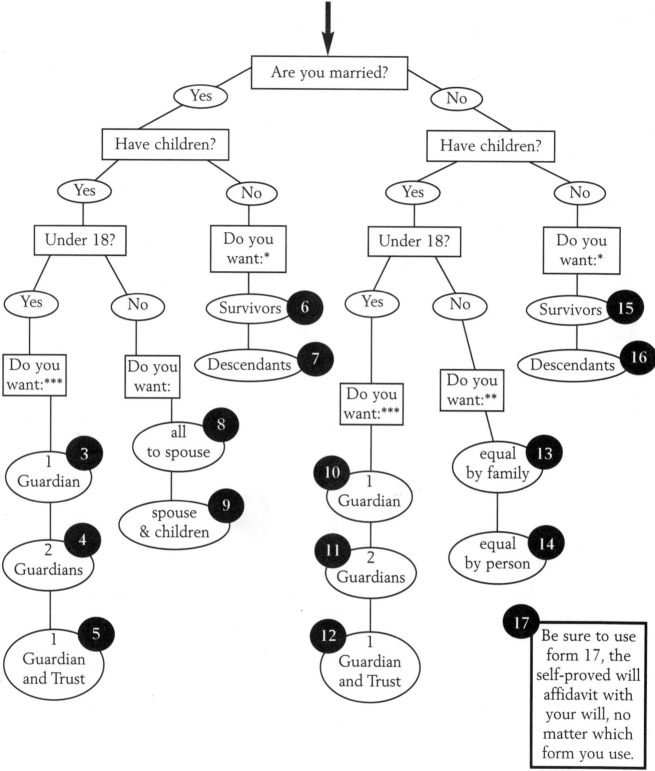

*For an explanation of survivors/descendants, see page 20.

**For an explanation of families/persons, see page 20.

*** For an explanation of childrens' guardians and trust, see pages 22-23.

Last Will and Testament

I, _____ a resident of _____
County, Georgia do hereby make, publish, and declare this to be my Last Will and Testament,
hereby revoking any and all Wills and Codicils heretofore made by me.

FIRST: I direct that all my just debts and funeral expenses be paid out of my estate as
soon after my death as is practicable.

SECOND: I give, devise, and bequeath the following specific gifts:

_____

_____

_____

_____

THIRD: I give, devise, and bequeath all my estate, real, personal, and mixed, of whatever kind and wherever situated, of which I may die seized or possessed, or in which I may
have any interest or over which I may have any power of appointment or testamentary disposition, to my spouse, _____. If my said spouse
does not survive me, I give, and bequeath the said property to my children _____

_____

_____,
plus any afterborn or adopted children in equal shares or their lineal descendants, per stirpes.

FOURTH: In the event that any beneficiary fails to survive me by thirty days, then
this will shall take effect as if that person had predeceased me.

FIFTH: Should my spouse not survive me, I hereby nominate, constitute, and appoint
_____, as guardian over the person of any of my children
who have not reached the age of majority at the time of my death. In the event that said
guardian is unable or unwilling to serve, then I nominate, constitute, and appoint _____
_____ as guardian. Said guardian shall serve without bond or surety.

SIXTH: Should my spouse not survive me, I hereby nominate, constitute, and appoint
_____ as guardian over the estate of any of my children who
have not reached the age of majority at the time of my death. In the event that said guardian
is unable or unwilling to serve, then I nominate, constitute, and appoint _____
_____ as guardian. Said guardian shall serve without bond or surety.

SEVENTH: I hereby nominate, constitute, and appoint _____
as Personal Representative of this, my Last Will and Testament. In the event that such named
person is unable or unwilling to serve at any time or for any reason, then I nominate, constitute, and appoint _____ as Personal Representative in the
place and stead of the person first named herein. It is my will and I direct that my Personal
Representative shall not be required to furnish a bond for the faithful performance of his or

Initials: _____ _____ _____   Page _1_ of ____
        Testator   Witness   Witness

her duties in any jurisdiction, any provision of law to the contrary notwithstanding, and I give my Personal Representative full power to administer my estate, including the power to settle claims, pay debts, and sell, lease or exchange real and personal property without court order.

IN WITNESS WHEREOF I declare this to be my Last Will and Testament and execute it willingly as my free and voluntary act for the purposes expressed herein and I am of legal age and sound mind and make this under no constraint or undue influence, this _____ day of _____, _____ at _____ State of _____.

_____L.S.

The foregoing instrument was on said date subscribed at the end thereof by _____, the above named Testator who signed, published, and declared this instrument to be his/her Last Will and Testament in the presence of us and each of us, who thereupon at his/her request, in his/her presence, and in the presence of each other, have hereunto subscribed our names as witnesses thereto. We are of sound mind and proper age to witness a will and understand this to be his/her will, and to the best of our knowledge testator is of legal age to make a will, of sound mind, and under no constraint or undue influence.

_____residing at_____

_____residing at_____

Last Will and Testament

I, _____ a resident of _____
County, Georgia do hereby make, publish, and declare this to be my Last Will and Testament,
hereby revoking any and all Wills and Codicils heretofore made by me.

FIRST: I direct that all my just debts and funeral expenses be paid out of my estate as
soon after my death as is practicable.

SECOND: I give, devise, and bequeath the following specific gifts:

_____

_____

_____

_____

THIRD: I give, devise, and bequeath all my estate, real, personal, and mixed, of whatever kind and wherever situated, of which I may die seized or possessed, or in which I may
have any interest or over which I may have any power of appointment or testamentary disposition, to my spouse, _____. If my said spouse
does not survive me, I give, and bequeath the said property to my children _____

_____

_____,
plus any afterborn or adopted children in equal shares or their lineal descendants, per stirpes.

FOURTH: In the event that any beneficiary fails to survive me by thirty days, then
this will shall take effect as if that person had predeceased me.

FIFTH: In the event that any of my children have not reached the age of _____
years at the time of my death, then the share of any such child shall be held in a separate
trust by _____ for such child.

The trustee shall use the income and that part of the principal of the trust as is, in the
trustee's sole discretion, necessary or desirable to provide proper housing, medical care, food,
clothing, entertainment and education for the trust beneficiary, considering the beneficiary's
other resources. Any income that is not distributed shall be added to the principal.
Additionally, the trustee shall have all powers conferred by the law of the state having jurisdiction over this trust, as well as the power to pay from the assets of the trust reasonable fees
necessary to administer the trust.

The trust shall terminate when the child reaches the age specified above and the remaining
assets distributed to the child, unless they have been exhausted sooner. In the event the child
dies prior to the termination of the trust, then the assets shall pass to the estate of the child.
The interests of the beneficiary under this trust shall not be assignable and shall be free from
the claims of creditors to the full extent allowed by law.

Initials: _____ _____ _____   Page _1_ of ____
    Testator   Witness   Witness

69

In the event the said trustee is unable or unwilling to serve for any reason, then I nominate, constitute, and appoint _____as alternate trustee. No bond shall be required of either trustee in any jurisdiction and this trust shall be administered without court supervision as allowed by law.

SIXTH: Should my spouse not survive me, I hereby nominate, constitute, and appoint _____as guardian over the person and estate of any of my children who have not reached the age of majority at the time of my death. In the event that said guardian is unable or unwilling to serve, then I nominate, constitute, and appoint _____ as guardian.

SEVENTH: I hereby nominate, constitute, and appoint _____ as Personal Representative of this, my Last Will and Testament. In the event that such named person is unable or unwilling to serve at any time or for any reason, then I nominate, constitute and appoint _____ as Personal Representative in the place and stead of the person first named herein. It is my will and I direct that my Personal Representative shall not be required to furnish a bond for the faithful performance of his or her duties in any jurisdiction, any provision of law to the contrary notwithstanding, and I give my Personal Representative full power to administer my estate, including the power to settle claims, pay debts, and sell, lease or exchange real and personal property without court order.

IN WITNESS WHEREOF I declare this to be my Last Will and Testament and execute it willingly as my free and voluntary act for the purposes expressed herein and I am of legal age and sound mind and make this under no constraint or undue influence, this _____ day of _____, _____ at _____ State of _____.

_____L.S.

The foregoing instrument was on said date subscribed at the end thereof by _____, the above named Testator who signed, published, and declared this instrument to be his/her Last Will and Testament in the presence of us and each of us, who thereupon at his/her request, in his/her presence, and in the presence of each other, have hereunto subscribed our names as witnesses thereto. We are of sound mind and proper age to witness a will and understand this to be his/her will, and to the best of our knowledge testator is of legal age to make a will, of sound mind, and under no constraint or undue influence.

_____residing at_____

_____residing at_____

Last Will and Testament

I, _____ a resident of _____
County, Georgia do hereby make, publish, and declare this to be my Last Will and Testament, hereby revoking any and all Wills and Codicils heretofore made by me.

FIRST: I direct that all my just debts and funeral expenses be paid out of my estate as soon after my death as is practicable.

SECOND: I give, devise, and bequeath the following specific gifts:

_____

_____

_____

_____

THIRD: I give, devise, and bequeath all my estate, real, personal, and mixed, of whatever kind and wherever situated, of which I may die seized or possessed, or in which I may have any interest or over which I may have any power of appointment or testamentary disposition, to my spouse, _____. If my said spouse does not survive me, I give, and bequeath the said property to _____

_____

_____,

or the survivor of them.

FOURTH: In the event that any beneficiary fails to survive me by thirty days, then this will shall take effect as if that person had predeceased me.

FIFTH: I hereby nominate, constitute, and appoint _____
as Personal Representative of this, my Last Will and Testament. In the event that such named person is unable or unwilling to serve at any time or for any reason, then I nominate, constitute, and appoint _____ as Personal Representative in the place and stead of the person first named herein. It is my will and I direct that my Personal Representative shall not be required to furnish a bond for the faithful performance of his or her duties in any jurisdiction, any provision of law to the contrary notwithstanding, and I give my Personal Representative full power to administer my estate, including the power to settle claims, pay debts, and sell, lease or exchange real and personal property without court order.

IN WITNESS WHEREOF I declare this to be my Last Will and Testament and execute it willingly as my free and voluntary act for the purposes expressed herein and I am of legal age and sound mind and make this under no constraint or undue influence, this _____ day of _____, _____ at _____ State of _____.

Initials: _____ _____ _____   Page __1__ of ____
      Testator   Witness   Witness

_____L.S.

    The foregoing instrument was on said date subscribed at the end thereof by _____, the above named Testator who signed, published, and declared this instrument to be his/her Last Will and Testament in the presence of us and each of us, who thereupon at his/her request, in his/her presence, and in the presence of each other, have hereunto subscribed our names as witnesses thereto. We are of sound mind and proper age to witness a will and understand this to be his/her will, and to the best of our knowledge testator is of legal age to make a will, of sound mind, and under no constraint or undue influence.

_____residing at_____

_____residing at_____

Last Will and Testament

I, _____ a resident of _____
County, Georgia do hereby make, publish, and declare this to be my Last Will and Testament,
hereby revoking any and all Wills and Codicils heretofore made by me.

FIRST: I direct that all my just debts and funeral expenses be paid out of my estate as
soon after my death as is practicable.

SECOND: I give, devise, and bequeath the following specific gifts:
_____
_____
_____
_____

THIRD: I give, devise, and bequeath all my estate, real, personal, and mixed, of whatever kind and wherever situated, of which I may die seized or possessed, or in which I may
have any interest or over which I may have any power of appointment or testamentary disposition, to my spouse, _____. If my said spouse
does not survive me, I give, and bequeath the said property to _____
_____
_____,
or to their lineal descendants, per stirpes.

FOURTH: In the event that any beneficiary fails to survive me by thirty days, then
this will shall take effect as if that person had predeceased me.

FIFTH: I hereby nominate, constitute, and appoint _____
as Personal Representative of this, my Last Will and Testament. In the event that such named
person is unable or unwilling to serve at any time or for any reason, then I nominate, constitute, and appoint _____ as Personal Representative in the
place and stead of the person first named herein. It is my will and I direct that my Personal
Representative shall not be required to furnish a bond for the faithful performance of his or
her duties in any jurisdiction, any provision of law to the contrary notwithstanding, and I give
my Personal Representative full power to administer my estate, including the power to settle claims, pay debts, and sell, lease or exchange real and personal property without court
order.

IN WITNESS WHEREOF I declare this to be my Last Will and Testament and execute it willingly as my free and voluntary act for the purposes expressed herein and I am of
legal age and sound mind and make this under no constraint or undue influence, this _____
day of _____, _____ at _____ State of _____.

Initials: _____ _____ _____   Page _1_ of _____
         Testator   Witness   Witness

_____L.S.

The foregoing instrument was on said date subscribed at the end thereof by _____, the above named Testator who signed, published, and declared this instrument to be his/her Last Will and Testament in the presence of us and each of us, who thereupon at his/her request, in his/her presence, and in the presence of each other, have hereunto subscribed our names as witnesses thereto. We are of sound mind and proper age to witness a will and understand this to be his/her will, and to the best of our knowledge testator is of legal age to make a will, of sound mind, and under no constraint or undue influence.

_____residing at_____

_____residing at_____

Last Will and Testament

I, _____ a resident of _____
County, Georgia do hereby make, publish, and declare this to be my Last Will and Testament, hereby revoking any and all Wills and Codicils heretofore made by me.

FIRST: I direct that all my just debts and funeral expenses be paid out of my estate as soon after my death as is practicable.

SECOND: I give, devise, and bequeath the following specific gifts:

_____

_____

_____

_____

THIRD: I give, devise, and bequeath all my estate, real, personal, and mixed, of whatever kind and wherever situated, of which I may die seized or possessed, or in which I may have any interest or over which I may have any power of appointment or testamentary disposition, to my spouse, _____. If my said spouse does not survive me, I give, and bequeath the said property to my children _____

_____

_____,
in equal shares or to their lineal descendants, per stirpes.

FOURTH: In the event that any beneficiary fails to survive me by thirty days, then this will shall take effect as if that person had predeceased me.

FIFTH: I hereby nominate, constitute, and appoint _____
as Personal Representative of this, my Last Will and Testament. In the event that such named person is unable or unwilling to serve at any time or for any reason, then I nominate, constitute, and appoint _____ as Personal Representative in the place and stead of the person first named herein. It is my will and I direct that my Personal Representative shall not be required to furnish a bond for the faithful performance of his or her duties in any jurisdiction, any provision of law to the contrary notwithstanding, and I give my Personal Representative full power to administer my estate, including the power to settle claims, pay debts, and sell, lease or exchange real and personal property without court order.

IN WITNESS WHEREOF I declare this to be my Last Will and Testament and execute it willingly as my free and voluntary act for the purposes expressed herein and I am of legal age and sound mind and make this under no constraint or undue influence, this _____ day of _____, _____ at _____ State of _____.

Initials: _____ _____ _____   Page _1_ of ____
         Testator   Witness   Witness

_____L.S.

The foregoing instrument was on said date subscribed at the end thereof by
_____, the above named Testator who signed, pub-
lished, and declared this instrument to be his/her Last Will and Testament in the presence of
us and each of us, who thereupon at his/her request, in his/her presence, and in the presence
of each other, have hereunto subscribed our names as witnesses thereto. We are of sound
mind and proper age to witness a will and understand this to be his/her will, and to the best
of our knowledge testator is of legal age to make a will, of sound mind, and under no constraint or undue influence.

_____residing at_____

_____residing at_____

Last Will and Testament

I, _____ a resident of _____ County, Georgia do hereby make, publish, and declare this to be my Last Will and Testament, hereby revoking any and all Wills and Codicils heretofore made by me.

FIRST: I direct that all my just debts and funeral expenses be paid out of my estate as soon after my death as is practicable.

SECOND: I give, devise, and bequeath the following specific gifts:

_____

_____

_____

_____

THIRD: I give, devise, and bequeath all my estate, real, personal, and mixed, of whatever kind and wherever situated, of which I may die seized or possessed, or in which I may have any interest or over which I may have any power of appointment or testamentary disposition, as follows:

_____% to my spouse, _____ and

_____% to my children, _____

_____

_____,

in equal shares or to their lineal descendants per stirpes.

FOURTH: In the event that any beneficiary fails to survive me by thirty days, then this will shall take effect as if that person had predeceased me.

FIFTH: I hereby nominate, constitute, and appoint _____ as Personal Representative of this, my Last Will and Testament. In the event that such named person is unable or unwilling to serve at any time or for any reason, then I nominate, constitute, and appoint _____ as Personal Representative in the place and stead of the person first named herein. It is my will and I direct that my Personal Representative shall not be required to furnish a bond for the faithful performance of his or her duties in any jurisdiction, any provision of law to the contrary notwithstanding, and I give my Personal Representative full power to administer my estate, including the power to settle claims, pay debts, and sell, lease or exchange real and personal property without court order.

IN WITNESS WHEREOF I declare this to be my Last Will and Testament and execute it willingly as my free and voluntary act for the purposes expressed herein and I am of legal age and sound mind and make this under no constraint or undue influence, this _____ day of _____, _____ at _____ State of _____.

Initials: _____ _____ _____
          Testator   Witness   Witness

Page _1_ of ____

_____L.S.

The foregoing instrument was on said date subscribed at the end thereof by _____, the above named Testator who signed, published, and declared this instrument to be his/her Last Will and Testament in the presence of us and each of us, who thereupon at his/her request, in his/her presence, and in the presence of each other, have hereunto subscribed our names as witnesses thereto. We are of sound mind and proper age to witness a will and understand this to be his/her will, and to the best of our knowledge testator is of legal age to make a will, of sound mind, and under no constraint or undue influence.

_____residing at_____

_____residing at_____

Last Will and Testament

I, _____ a resident of _____ County, Georgia do hereby make, publish, and declare this to be my Last Will and Testament, hereby revoking any and all Wills and Codicils heretofore made by me.

FIRST: I direct that all my just debts and funeral expenses be paid out of my estate as soon after my death as is practicable.

SECOND: I give, devise, and bequeath the following specific gifts:

_____

_____

_____

_____

THIRD: I give, devise, and bequeath all my estate, real, personal, and mixed, of whatever kind and wherever situated, of which I may die seized or possessed, or in which I may have any interest or over which I may have any power of appointment or testamentary disposition, to my children _____

_____

_____,

plus any afterborn or adopted children in equal shares or to their lineal descendants per stirpes.

FOURTH: In the event that any beneficiary fails to survive me by thirty days, then this will shall take effect as if that person had predeceased me.

FIFTH: In the event any of my children have not attained the age of 18 years at the time of my death, I hereby nominate, constitute, and appoint _____ as guardian over the person of any of my children who have not reached the age of majority at the time of my death. In the event that said guardian is unable or unwilling to serve, then I nominate, constitute, and appoint _____ as guardian. Said guardian shall serve without bond or surety.

SIXTH: In the event any of my children have not attained the age of 18 years at the time of my death, I hereby nominate, constitute, and appoint _____ as guardian over the estate of any of my children who have not reached the age of majority at the time of my death. In the event that said guardian is unable or unwilling to serve, then I nominate, constitute, and appoint _____ as guardian. Said guardian shall serve without bond or surety.

SEVENTH: I hereby nominate, constitute, and appoint _____ as Personal Representative of this, my Last Will and Testament. In the event that such named person is unable or unwilling to serve at any time or for any reason, then I nominate, consti-

Initials: _____ _____ _____   Page _1_ of ____

      Testator   Witness   Witness

tute, and appoint _____ as Personal Representative in the place and stead of the person first named herein. It is my will and I direct that my Personal Representative shall not be required to furnish a bond for the faithful performance of his or her duties in any jurisdiction, any provision of law to the contrary notwithstanding, and I give my Personal Representative full power to administer my estate, including the power to settle claims, pay debts, and sell, lease or exchange real and personal property without court order.

IN WITNESS WHEREOF I declare this to be my Last Will and Testament and execute it willingly as my free and voluntary act for the purposes expressed herein and I am of legal age and sound mind and make this under no constraint or undue influence, this _____ day of _____, _____ at _____ State of _____.

_____L.S.

The foregoing instrument was on said date subscribed at the end thereof by _____, the above named Testator who signed, published, and declared this instrument to be his/her Last Will and Testament in the presence of us and each of us, who thereupon at his/her request, in his/her presence, and in the presence of each other, have hereunto subscribed our names as witnesses thereto. We are of sound mind and proper age to witness a will and understand this to be his/her will, and to the best of our knowledge testator is of legal age to make a will, of sound mind, and under no constraint or undue influence.

_____residing at_____

_____residing at_____

Last Will and Testament

I, _____ a resident of _____ County, Georgia do hereby make, publish, and declare this to be my Last Will and Testament, hereby revoking any and all Wills and Codicils heretofore made by me.

FIRST: I direct that all my just debts and funeral expenses be paid out of my estate as soon after my death as is practicable.

SECOND: I give, devise, and bequeath the following specific gifts:

_____

_____

_____

THIRD: I give, devise, and bequeath all my estate, real, personal, and mixed, of whatever kind and wherever situated, of which I may die seized or possessed, or in which I may have any interest or over which I may have any power of appointment or testamentary disposition, to my children _____

_____

_____,

plus any afterborn or adopted children in equal shares or to their lineal descendants per stirpes.

FOURTH: In the event that any beneficiary fails to survive me by thirty days, then this will shall take effect as if that person had predeceased me.

FIFTH: In the event that any of my children have not reached the age of _____ years at the time of my death, then the share of any such child shall be held in a separate trust by _____ for such child.

The trustee shall use the income and that part of the principal of the trust as is, in the trustee's sole discretion, necessary or desirable to provide proper housing, medical care, food, clothing, entertainment and education for the trust beneficiary, considering the beneficiary's other resources. Any income that is not distributed shall be added to the principal. Additionally, the trustee shall have all powers conferred by the law of the state having jurisdiction over this trust, as well as the power to pay from the assets of the trust reasonable fees necessary to administer the trust.

The trust shall terminate when the child reaches the age specified above and the remaining assets distributed to the child, unless they have been exhausted sooner. In the event the child dies prior to the termination of the trust, then the assets shall pass to the estate of the child. The interests of the beneficiary under this trust shall not be assignable and shall be free from the claims of creditors to the full extent allowed by law.

In the event the said trustee is unable or unwilling to serve for any reason, then I nominate, constitute, and appoint _____as alternate trustee. No bond shall be required of either trustee in any jurisdiction and this trust shall be administered without court supervision as allowed by law.

Initials: _____ _____ _____   Page __1__ of ____

Testator   Witness   Witness

SIXTH: In the event any of my children have not attained the age of 18 years at the time of my death, I hereby nominate, constitute, and appoint _____ as guardian over the person and estate of any of my children who have not reached the age of majority at the time of my death. In the event that said guardian is unable or unwilling to serve, then I nominate, constitute, and appoint _____ as guardian. Said guardian shall serve without bond or surety.

SEVENTH: I hereby nominate, constitute, and appoint _____ as Personal Representative of this, my Last Will and Testament. In the event that such named person is unable or unwilling to serve at any time or for any reason, then I nominate, constitute, and appoint _____ as Personal Representative in the place and stead of the person first named herein. It is my will and I direct that my Personal Representative shall not be required to furnish a bond for the faithful performance of his or her duties in any jurisdiction, any provision of law to the contrary notwithstanding, and I give my Personal Representative full power to administer my estate, including the power to settle claims, pay debts, and sell, lease or exchange real and personal property without court order.

IN WITNESS WHEREOF I declare this to be my Last Will and Testament and execute it willingly as my free and voluntary act for the purposes expressed herein and I am of legal age and sound mind and make this under no constraint or undue influence, this _____ day of _____, _____ at _____ State of _____.

_____L.S.

The foregoing instrument was on said date subscribed at the end thereof by _____, the above named Testator who signed, published, and declared this instrument to be his/her Last Will and Testament in the presence of us and each of us, who thereupon at his/her request, in his/her presence, and in the presence of each other, have hereunto subscribed our names as witnesses thereto. We are of sound mind and proper age to witness a will and understand this to be his/her will, and to the best of our knowledge testator is of legal age to make a will, of sound mind, and under no constraint or undue influence.

_____residing at_____

_____residing at_____

Page _2_ of ____

Last Will and Testament

I, _____ a resident of _____ County, Georgia do hereby make, publish, and declare this to be my Last Will and Testament, hereby revoking any and all Wills and Codicils heretofore made by me.

FIRST: I direct that all my just debts and funeral expenses be paid out of my estate as soon after my death as is practicable.

SECOND: I give, devise, and bequeath the following specific gifts:

_____

_____

_____

_____

THIRD: I give, devise, and bequeath all my estate, real, personal, and mixed, of whatever kind and wherever situated, of which I may die seized or possessed, or in which I may have any interest or over which I may have any power of appointment or testamentary disposition, to my children _____

_____

_____,

in equal shares, or their lineal descendants per stirpes.

FOURTH: In the event that any beneficiary fails to survive me by thirty days, then this will shall take effect as if that person had predeceased me.

FIFTH: I hereby nominate, constitute, and appoint _____ as Personal Representative of this, my Last Will and Testament. In the event that such named person is unable or unwilling to serve at any time or for any reason, then I nominate, constitute, and appoint _____ as Personal Representative in the place and stead of the person first named herein. It is my will and I direct that my Personal Representative shall not be required to furnish a bond for the faithful performance of his or her duties in any jurisdiction, any provision of law to the contrary notwithstanding, and I give my Personal Representative full power to administer my estate, including the power to settle claims, pay debts, and sell, lease or exchange real and personal property without court order.

IN WITNESS WHEREOF I declare this to be my Last Will and Testament and execute it willingly as my free and voluntary act for the purposes expressed herein and I am of legal age and sound mind and make this under no constraint or undue influence, this _____ day of _____, _____ at _____ State of _____.

Initials: _____ _____ _____

Testator   Witness   Witness

Page 1 of ____

85

_____L.S.

    The foregoing instrument was on said date subscribed at the end thereof by _____, the above named Testator who signed, published, and declared this instrument to be his/her Last Will and Testament in the presence of us and each of us, who thereupon at his/her request, in his/her presence, and in the presence of each other, have hereunto subscribed our names as witnesses thereto. We are of sound mind and proper age to witness a will and understand this to be his/her will, and to the best of our knowledge testator is of legal age to make a will, of sound mind, and under no constraint or undue influence.

_____residing at_____

_____residing at_____

Page __2__ of ____

Last Will and Testament

I, _____ a resident of _____ County, Georgia do hereby make, publish, and declare this to be my Last Will and Testament, hereby revoking any and all Wills and Codicils heretofore made by me.

FIRST: I direct that all my just debts and funeral expenses be paid out of my estate as soon after my death as is practicable.

SECOND: I give, devise, and bequeath the following specific gifts:

_____

_____

_____

_____

THIRD: I give, devise, and bequeath all my estate, real, personal, and mixed, of whatever kind and wherever situated, of which I may die seized or possessed, or in which I may have any interest or over which I may have any power of appointment or testamentary disposition, to my children _____

_____

_____,

in equal shares, or their lineal descendants per capita.

FOURTH: In the event that any beneficiary fails to survive me by thirty days, then this will shall take effect as if that person had predeceased me.

FIFTH: I hereby nominate, constitute, and appoint _____ as Personal Representative of this, my Last Will and Testament. In the event that such named person is unable or unwilling to serve at any time or for any reason, then I nominate, constitute, and appoint _____ as Personal Representative in the place and stead of the person first named herein. It is my will and I direct that my Personal Representative shall not be required to furnish a bond for the faithful performance of his or her duties in any jurisdiction, any provision of law to the contrary notwithstanding, and I give my Personal Representative full power to administer my estate, including the power to settle claims, pay debts, and sell, lease or exchange real and personal property without court order.

IN WITNESS WHEREOF I declare this to be my Last Will and Testament and execute it willingly as my free and voluntary act for the purposes expressed herein and I am of legal age and sound mind and make this under no constraint or undue influence, this _____ day of _____, _____ at _____ State of _____.

Initials: _____ _____ _____   Page _1_ of _____
        Testator   Witness   Witness

_____L.S.

The foregoing instrument was on said date subscribed at the end thereof by
_____, the above named Testator who signed, published, and declared this instrument to be his/her Last Will and Testament in the presence of us and each of us, who thereupon at his/her request, in his/her presence, and in the presence of each other, have hereunto subscribed our names as witnesses thereto. We are of sound mind and proper age to witness a will and understand this to be his/her will, and to the best of our knowledge testator is of legal age to make a will, of sound mind, and under no constraint or undue influence.

_____residing at_____

_____residing at_____

Last Will and Testament

I, _____ a resident of _____ County, Georgia do hereby make, publish, and declare this to be my Last Will and Testament, hereby revoking any and all Wills and Codicils heretofore made by me.

FIRST: I direct that all my just debts and funeral expenses be paid out of my estate as soon after my death as is practicable.

SECOND: I give, devise, and bequeath the following specific gifts:

_____

_____

_____

_____

THIRD: I give, devise, and bequeath all my estate, real, personal, and mixed, of whatever kind and wherever situated, of which I may die seized or possessed, or in which I may have any interest or over which I may have any power of appointment or testamentary disposition, to the following: _____

_____

_____,

or to the survivor of them.

FOURTH: In the event that any beneficiary fails to survive me by thirty days, then this will shall take effect as if that person had predeceased me.

FIFTH: I hereby nominate, constitute, and appoint _____ as Personal Representative of this, my Last Will and Testament. In the event that such named person is unable or unwilling to serve at any time or for any reason, then I nominate, constitute, and appoint _____ as Personal Representative in the place and stead of the person first named herein. It is my will and I direct that my Personal Representative shall not be required to furnish a bond for the faithful performance of his or her duties in any jurisdiction, any provision of law to the contrary notwithstanding, and I give my Personal Representative full power to administer my estate, including the power to settle claims, pay debts, and sell, lease or exchange real and personal property without court order.

IN WITNESS WHEREOF I declare this to be my Last Will and Testament and execute it willingly as my free and voluntary act for the purposes expressed herein and I am of legal age and sound mind and make this under no constraint or undue influence, this _____ day of _____, _____ at _____ State of _____.

Initials: _____ _____ _____   Page _1_ of ____
      Testator   Witness   Witness

_____L.S.

The foregoing instrument was on said date subscribed at the end thereof by _____, the above named Testator who signed, published, and declared this instrument to be his/her Last Will and Testament in the presence of us and each of us, who thereupon at his/her request, in his/her presence, and in the presence of each other, have hereunto subscribed our names as witnesses thereto. We are of sound mind and proper age to witness a will and understand this to be his/her will, and to the best of our knowledge testator is of legal age to make a will, of sound mind, and under no constraint or undue influence.

_____residing at_____

_____residing at_____

Page __2__ of ____

Last Will and Testament

I, _____ a resident of _____

County, Georgia do hereby make, publish, and declare this to be my Last Will and Testament, hereby revoking any and all Wills and Codicils heretofore made by me.

FIRST: I direct that all my just debts and funeral expenses be paid out of my estate as soon after my death as is practicable.

SECOND: I give, devise, and bequeath the following specific gifts:

_____

_____

_____

_____

THIRD: I give, devise, and bequeath all my estate, real, personal, and mixed, of whatever kind and wherever situated, of which I may die seized or possessed, or in which I may have any interest or over which I may have any power of appointment or testamentary disposition, to the following _____

_____

_____,

in equal shares, or their lineal descendants per stirpes.

FOURTH: In the event that any beneficiary fails to survive me by thirty days, then this will shall take effect as if that person had predeceased me.

FIFTH: I hereby nominate, constitute, and appoint _____ as Personal Representative of this, my Last Will and Testament. In the event that such named person is unable or unwilling to serve at any time or for any reason, then I nominate, constitute, and appoint _____ as Personal Representative in the place and stead of the person first named herein. It is my will and I direct that my Personal Representative shall not be required to furnish a bond for the faithful performance of his or her duties in any jurisdiction, any provision of law to the contrary notwithstanding, and I give my Personal Representative full power to administer my estate, including the power to settle claims, pay debts, and sell, lease or exchange real and personal property without court order.

IN WITNESS WHEREOF I declare this to be my Last Will and Testament and execute it willingly as my free and voluntary act for the purposes expressed herein and I am of legal age and sound mind and make this under no constraint or undue influence, this _____ day of _____, _____ at _____ State of _____.

Initials: _____ _____ _____   Page _1_ of ____

     Testator   Witness   Witness

_____L.S.

The foregoing instrument was on said date subscribed at the end thereof by _____, the above named Testator who signed, published, and declared this instrument to be his/her Last Will and Testament in the presence of us and each of us, who thereupon at his/her request, in his/her presence, and in the presence of each other, have hereunto subscribed our names as witnesses thereto. We are of sound mind and proper age to witness a will and understand this to be his/her will, and to the best of our knowledge testator is of legal age to make a will, of sound mind, and under no constraint or undue influence.

_____residing at_____

_____residing at_____

Page __2__ of ____

UNIFORM DONOR CARD

The undersigned hereby makes this anatomical gift, if medically acceptable, to take effect on death. The words and marks below indicate my desires:

I give:

      (a) _____ any needed organs or parts;

      (b) _____ only the following organs or parts

_____

for the purpose of transplantation, therapy, medical research, or education;

      (c) _____ my body for anatomical study if needed.

Limitations or special wishes, if any:

_____

Signed by the donor and the following witnesses in the presence of each other:

_____	_____
Signature of Donor	Date of birth
_____	_____
Date signed	City & State
_____	_____
Witness	Witness
_____	_____
Address	Address

UNIFORM DONOR CARD

The undersigned hereby makes this anatomical gift, if medically acceptable, to take effect on death. The words and marks below indicate my desires:

I give:

      (a) _____ any needed organs or parts;

      (b) _____ only the following organs or parts

_____

for the purpose of transplantation, therapy, medical research, or education;

      (c) _____ my body for anatomical study if needed.

Limitations or special wishes, if any:

_____

Signed by the donor and the following witnesses in the presence of each other:

_____	_____
Signature of Donor	Date of birth
_____	_____
Date signed	City & State
_____	_____
Witness	Witness
_____	_____
Address	Address

UNIFORM DONOR CARD

The undersigned hereby makes this anatomical gift, if medically acceptable, to take effect on death. The words and marks below indicate my desires:

I give:

      (a) _____ any needed organs or parts;

      (b) _____ only the following organs or parts

_____

for the purpose of transplantation, therapy, medical research, or education;

      (c) _____ my body for anatomical study if needed.

Limitations or special wishes, if any:

_____

Signed by the donor and the following witnesses in the presence of each other:

_____	_____
Signature of Donor	Date of birth
_____	_____
Date signed	City & State
_____	_____
Witness	Witness
_____	_____
Address	Address

UNIFORM DONOR CARD

The undersigned hereby makes this anatomical gift, if medically acceptable, to take effect on death. The words and marks below indicate my desires:

I give:

      (a) _____ any needed organs or parts;

      (b) _____ only the following organs or parts

_____

for the purpose of transplantation, therapy, medical research, or education;

      (c) _____ my body for anatomical study if needed.

Limitations or special wishes, if any:

_____

Signed by the donor and the following witnesses in the presence of each other:

_____	_____
Signature of Donor	Date of birth
_____	_____
Date signed	City & State
_____	_____
Witness	Witness
_____	_____
Address	Address

One of these cards should be cut out and carried in your wallet or purse.

Index

Sphinx® Publishing's National Titles

Valid in All 50 States

Legal Survival in Business

The Complete Book of Corporate Forms	$24.95
How to Form a Delaware Corporation from Any State	$24.95
How to Form a Limited Liability Company	$22.95
Incorporate in Nevada from Any State	$24.95
How to Form a Nonprofit Corporation	$24.95
How to Form Your Own Corporation (3E)	$24.95
How to Form Your Own Partnership	$22.95
How to Register Your Own Copyright (3E)	$21.95
How to Register Your Own Trademark (3E)	$21.95
Most Valuable Business Legal Forms You'll Ever Need (3E)	$21.95

Legal Survival in Court

Crime Victim's Guide to Justice (2E)	$21.95
Grandparents' Rights (3E)	$24.95
Help Your Lawyer Win Your Case (2E)	$14.95
Jurors' Rights (2E)	$12.95
Legal Research Made Easy (2E)	$16.95
Winning Your Personal Injury Claim (2E)	$24.95
Your Rights When You Owe Too Much	$16.95

Legal Survival in Real Estate

Essential Guide to Real Estate Contracts	$18.95
Essential Guide to Real Estate Leases	$18.95
How to Buy a Condominium or Townhome (2E)	$19.95

Legal Survival in Personal Affairs

Cómo Hacer su Propio Testamento	$16.95
Guía de Inmigración a Estados Unidos (3E)	$24.95
Guía de Justicia para Víctimas del Crimen	$21.95
Cómo Solicitar su Propio Divorcio	$24.95
How to File Your Own Bankruptcy (5E)	$21.95
How to File Your Own Divorce (4E)	$24.95
How to Make Your Own Will (2E)	$16.95
How to Write Your Own Living Will (2E)	$16.95
How to Write Your Own Premarital Agreement (3E)	$24.95
How to Win Your Unemployment Compensation Claim	$21.95
Living Trusts and Simple Ways to Avoid Probate (2E)	$22.95
Manual de Beneficios para el Seguro Social	$18.95
Most Valuable Personal Legal Forms You'll Ever Need	$24.95
Neighbor v. Neighbor (2E)	$16.95
The Nanny and Domestic Help Legal Kit	$22.95
The Power of Attorney Handbook (3E)	$19.95
Repair Your Own Credit and Deal with Debt	$18.95
The Social Security Benefits Handbook (3E)	$18.95
Unmarried Parents' Rights	$19.95
U.S.A. Immigration Guide (3E)	$19.95
Your Right to Child Custody, Visitation and Support (2E)	$24.95

Legal Survival Guides are directly available from Sourcebooks, Inc., or from your local bookstores.
Prices are subject to change without notice.

For credit card orders call 1–800–432–7444, write P.O. Box 4410, Naperville, IL 60567-4410
or fax 630-961-2168